Winning Without Losing Your Way

Character-Centered Leadership

Rebecca Barnett

Dedication

This book is for sensei who did not falter. Rachelle, my north star, and for Nora Mae who taught me true courage.

Advance praise for *Winning Without Losing Your Way: Character-centered Leadership.*

This is a wonderful book for any professional interested in improving their leadership skills and characteristics. The author does an excellent job of presenting today's business environment and relating life experiences to leadership capabilities. I really enjoyed reading the insights from so many of today's leaders.

Ann Drake
Chief Executive Officer, DSC Logistics

Winning does a superb job of bringing to life core values like honor, integrity, and character through personal stories of both ordinary and extraordinary individuals. It is an excellent read for everyone, but especially for those at a crossroads in their life.

Jimmy Pedro
Three-time Olympian
1999 World Champion

Teachers, preachers, supervisors, coaches, prosecutors and a host of others whose daily decisions affect the lives of others should take the time to read this concise philosophy of what personal character means in leadership. The author has captured a means to self inventory and examination without empty mysticism or meaningless buzzwords. I am recommending this book to the attorney's I supervise; its lessons provide a lens to magnify the moral core of every decision we face.

Joseph Owmby
Assistant District Attorney
Harris County Texas

If you manage any people or make decisions of any consequence in your organization, you should read this book. The ideas expressed reinforce the values and ethics that most of us already share. It serves as a practical reminder of our role in building a culture in our organizations that we can be proud of.

Trevor Hanlon
CPFR/Forecast Manager
Clorox Sales Company

Displaying character and highlighting virtues are finally entering the workplace and Rebecca Barnett's timing with this insightful book couldn't be better. Displaying her personal integrity, she weaves stories and interviews to help the reader choose what is best for their career decisions.

Sandra Ford Walston
Author of Courage, the heart and spirit of every woman

This book will be a gift to many people. Rebecca has achieved the seemingly impossible. She has written a business book that provokes your thinking and encourages your heart. It is a must read for today's leaders faced with ethical challenges. The book, like its author, is packed full of energy and information. It is sure to become a valuable resource for all current and future leaders.

Lisa Williams PhD.
Professor of Marketing and Transportation
Walton College of Business Administration
University of Arkansas

Rebecca speaks with the heart of someone who knows her topic first hand. In today's business environment, the companies which can keep, or can win back, the loyalty of their people will be successful to a much greater degree than those who can not. Paying heed to what Rebecca says can definitely help companies win the loyalty of their people.

Tom Koentop
Director, Professional Services
Lee Hecht Harrison

Rebecca is a powerful voice for getting to the heart of truth. And, it is through her integrity within her written words that we can all benefit and learn from. I recommend this book for anyone struggling with choice in their personal or professional lives.

Vanessa Wynn
President, Shy Hill Marketing

The content of this publication comes from the depths of the soul of someone who knows; someone who has done the research on leadership styles. *Winning* is a must-read by anyone searching for the latest insights and character of successful leadership.

Juanell Teague
President, People Plus

Rebecca Barnett's book is for anyone who has ever examined his or her direction in life. Through retelling of poignant stories of successes and failures, both personal and professional, Rebecca allows us to explore our own attitudes and values. Her book opens one up to keeping values and work/life balance in perspective.

Louise Durej
Hartford Life

I have always believed that it must be possible to lead without compromising my personal values and integrity. After I recently made the "right" decision, and it cost me my job, I happened to find Rebecca and her book. She helped me see that it was courage, and not stupidity, that made me willing to risk my job. I wish I'd had her examples and insights to turn to years ago – I would have agonized less and made my decision sooner!

Emily G. Rodriguez,
VP Program Management
EBoomerang, Inc.

This book would appeal to anyone who works regardless of industry...it asks the hard questions that confront you when your career hits a speed bump or that creep out in the wee hours about work and family balance....it could be the answer for how to get back on the right track to live fully and with fulfillment. Read it once AND then re-read it annually to keep the lessons fresh!

Nancy Haslip
Managing Director Shared Services
FleetBoston Financial

Winning is a book of core fundamentals that any person should read as they look to incorporate values into their life and their work. Sometimes we forget the little things that mean so much when dealing with people and all the complexities of the world we live in. This book is a great reminder of what is truly important in life. Enjoyable and very relative reading.

Tim Barber
Executive VP Sales & Marketing
Expeditors

I think that it would be beneficial for managers as well as the students aspiring to become managers to read this. They should understand that having the courage to do what is right is more widespread than newspaper headlines would have them think!

Bernie Hale
Principal, Hale Logistics Consulting

If I had heard from the people and considered the issues in Rebecca's book at the beginning of my career, my life planning would have been different. What you want when you are 25 is vastly different from what you want at 45; but you need to plan for 45 at 25. If you are already established, many of the experiences in the book will resonate personally. The experiences and questions will help you evaluate and create personal change.

Catherine Weeks
Global Transportation and Compliance
Taylor Made Adidas Golf Company

Business people seldom think about values in their day to day activities. That's a shame because they could make those around them more efficient if they took the time to instill organizational values and respect the values that colleagues bring to the relationship. This book does an excellent job of getting managers to see ourselves as others see us . . . and to see others pretty much in the way that they would like to be seen.

George A. Gecowets
Executive Vice President (Retired)
Council of Logistics Management

As we live and work in a world whose ethical compass is seemingly dysfunctional, *Winning* offers us the insights and example of a host of honorable people in leadership roles. It also reminds us that leadership is found at all levels of an organization. And, with individual commitment to integrity and an ethical code of conduct we can shape a better world in which to live and work. *Winning* should be required reading for any leadership development program.

Clint Brizendine
Rehabilitation Technology Coordinator
Kentucky State Government

The insight provided through executive anecdotes and Rebecca's personal experiences with ethics in business, in life, speak to the profound need for greater awareness of accountability for our own lives and actions. Our choices do matter and have impact. Winning without Losing Your Way shows just how much."

Wendy Tarzian
President, Tarzian Search Consultants, Inc.

Rebecca Barnett has written a powerful book that addresses an issue of importance to all of us. How do I live a full, meaningful and balanced life? Drawing on her rich and varied experiences as a successful manager, athlete, wife, and mother, along with those of leaders in various fields, she provides some rich insights into this vexing question. As you read this book, you will come away with a set of valuable principles to achieve this elusive goal. Of particular relevance is her focus on courage, character and integrity. During these troubled times, this is a book that will provide you with a solid grounding in what is truly important in life.

Dan Goodwill
President, Dan Goodwill & Associates

Winning is a book for all business leaders, no matter the industry, it teaches us about the qualities it takes to be a true leader. Rebecca's book allows you to educate yourself on trust, integrity and reliability. It is a thoroughly enjoyable read, entertaining while it educates.

Fran Chargar
Executive Vice President
Logistics Horizons LLC

It's 3:00 a.m. and I am reading email in Shanghi – talk about needing balance! Rebecca's book causes you to rethink decisions you made so long ago. I am sending my son, a recent MBA from Vanderbilt, a copy in hopes that it is not too late for him.

David Miles
Global Sourcing Retail
Dollar General

Thanks for helping me to understand the various generations within an organization. No wonder I am tired. I would gladly recommend the book not only to senior management but to young professionals who find themselves in a "melting pot" corporate culture where they are trying to make a difference.

Harriett Seward
Senior Logistics Project Manager
Ryder Logistics and Transportation Worldwide

When thrust into leadership roles ordinary people often lose their way. Whether it is in business or our community we sometimes find that "it's a jungle out there." Cutting a path through the undergrowth by sharing stories of courage, character, and balance, If we are to find our way as leaders, this is the kind of direction we need.

Neil Ohlenkamp
Founder Judo Information Site

Rebecca Barnett's work represents a timely collection of stories reflecting the heart and soul of Character-Centered Leadership. *Winning* is filled with reminders of our individual journey to live core values and build commitment for excellence in leadership in others.

Ted Fancher
Leader, Tower Automotive University
Tower Automotive

America is an amazing nation which has been historically blessed with character-centered leadership from its inception to the current era both in the public and the private sectors. Current lapses in corporate and government behavior beg for a return to what is at the core of American success, responsible and ethical individual behavior. All the laws and reforms will be for nothing without individuals accepting the responsibility of doing the next right thing. This is not always simple or easy to discern or accomplish.

Winning provides insights to us all about what really is important at the end of the day, week, month, year, and life time.

James S. Bregman
President, Deco International, Ltd.
1964 first Olympic Judo team

Rebecca blends the real world with character in leadership and there is no replacement for integrity and creditability. In the final analysis we are all only pencilled in and having these leadership traits are what allows greatness.

William Parsons
Executive Professor, International Business
Office of Global business and entrepreneurship
Western Kentucky University

Through personal stories and stories that Rebecca gathered in countless interviews, we are encouraged to look deep inside and discover how we would define success, character, integrity, and courage; whether or not we have balance in our lives; and if given the opportunity, what life-skill encouragement would we give our children and others looking for help and advice. This book will make you think and come to grips with who you are, who you want to be, and how you can make a difference in the world around you.

John Pavleje
Author of Leadership ... Because You Care!

I was impressed and appreciated the collection of stories. I am moved and humbled by the different individual struggles that people faced and how they faced them.

Tim Duffy
Principle
Duffy Supply Chain Consulting Services

Here's the book that everybody wishes they had read years ago. It helps you put the right perspective on what matters in a career.

Bob Vines
Lexmark

Winning Without Losing Your Way

Character-Centered Leadership

Contents

A first word to readers

There are too many people who have encouraged and advised me to thank publicly. Let me begin by thanking my parents, who provided an early grounding in values and modeled a happy marriage. Special thanks to my editor, Helen Richardson, who helped me find my voice.

I am deeply appreciative of the men and women who shared their experiences even when they were unflattering or deeply personal in the hopes that it would help someone else. These are their stories, their voices. My role is to tell it true.

After years of living close to the country music capital, I have learned that the rare, great country song captures a moment, encapsulating it in emotion and meaning and melody. The same is true with each quote chosen to complement a section. I can hear music. If you listen closely, you can hear it too.

Early in the incubation stages of this book, I asked Cumberland College Coach, Doug Fortune, why there were so many books on the "how to" of judo, but none of the "why". He told me that judo is like faith, unique and individual for each. I thought about it and realized that was all the more reason to write.

I owe a great debt to the American judo community: the referees who give up weekends with their family to ensure the right competitor wins, the coaches who develop the next generation of Olympians without pay or recognition, and especially the athletes, who bedazzle us with their breathtaking courage and athleticism.

January 2003 marks three years since I began my journey with one burning question. For a long while the book didn't seem possible. After the first year of research and interviews I had compiled a stack of paperwork that towered above my head. The stories and quotes from interview participants jostled and jockeyed for position, drowning out my voice. I made several attempts to write, but the task was overwhelming and I put the book aside.

On September 11th, the world shifted on its axis. For two days I sat glued to the television, mesmerized by the images of falling towers and the stories of great courage and unspeakable loss.

On the third day I began to write. The trauma of 9/11 brought into sharp focus the life lessons of the interview participants and the urgency of this message.

I completed the manuscript as a summer of accounting scandals shook our corporations. I worried that the book would be misperceived as capitalizing on other's misfortune, but a friend of deep faith reassured me. He said, "God has smiled on you."

He has.

Foreword

Sports are often used as a shorthand analogy for life. There are stories of failure and redemption, of victory and defeat. But the sports event itself is a small part of the larger issue of how we live our lives.

The judo community in the United States is small - only 15,000 athletes by most estimates - and closely knit. We see each other at our best and at our worst, at our most vulnerable times, when we are injured, discouraged, losing. Over years of competition, we become bonded by sweat and blood.

We lost three athletes in the attack on America of September 11th, 2002. Two were firefighters; Paul Pansini, a bronze medalist in the World Police and Fire Games and Christian Reganhard, a brown belt with the bright promise of a competitive career. And we lost our 1992 National Collegiate Champion, Jeremy Glick.

About an hour into United Flight #93, from Newark to San Francisco, Jeremy called his wife and high school sweetheart, Lyzbeth, from the plane. He told her that his plane had been hijacked by three terrorists wearing red headbands and wielding knives. Claiming the red box strapped around one terrorist's waist was a bomb, they had taken over the cockpit, and forced passengers to the rear of the plane.

Jeremy heard another passenger report a plane had hit the World Trade Center. He asked Lyz if it were true, trying to grasp what had happened. When, near Cleveland, the plane took a hard turn south, on course for Washington D.C., he knew that his flight was not going to make it to safety.

But Jeremy had a plan with two other men to take on the terrorists and he wanted her blessing. Lyz told him, "Do whatever you can."

During that five minute phone conversation they said, "I love you 1,000 times." Lyz heard the sadness in Jeremy's voice, but he told her to have a good life and be happy.

Lyz said, "Put a picture of me and Emmy in your head - be strong and brave." Jeremy kept the cell phone on, but she could not bear to hear the struggle.

Moments later United Flight 93 crashed in the rolling fields of rural Western Pennsylvania, killing everyone on board. Jeremy lived as he died - without fear, with honor and with courage.

Now, even as we grieve, we are proud. And we are so grateful. Lyz said, "I think God had this larger purpose for him. He was supposed to fly out the night before, but couldn't. I had Emmy one month early, so Jeremy got to see her. You can't tell me God isn't at work there."

In October, at the 2001 U.S. Open Judo Championships, our three brave men were honored in the evening opening ceremonies. Earlier in the day, elimination rounds of competition were flat. The competitors felt cheated by the many missing athletes whose countries were afraid to send them to the United States. We struggled through the competition rounds, wanting to do right by the athletes.

Opening ceremonies were somber, the mats empty. There wasn't a colorful parade of country flags. The athletes didn't march in. The hall was silent without warm up music. There was only one small table in the center of the mats. It held three Gold Medals of Honor and a loosely circled black belt.

Two young men dressed like rappers sang a hauntingly beautiful Star Spangled Banner. We stood, hands on heart and blinked back tears as our three men were awarded Gold Medals of Honor. Jeremy Glick was awarded the highest possible honor in judo, a 10th degree black belt.

The next morning, I talked to Jeremy's coach. In his 34-year coaching career, Sensei Ogasawara produced many national judo champions. His daughter Liliko became an Olympian, winning silver and bronze medals in the World Championships. He coached two-time Olympian, Celita Schutz. And he trained Jeremy Glick. Sensei Ogasawara said, "Jeremy was 7 years old when he started judo, but he never cried like the other children. He was strong physically and mentally. Jeremy was not afraid."

Sometimes, we are afraid. But courage is not the absence of fear. Rather, it is stepping out in faith in the face of fear. Sometimes, as managers we get so caught up in competition that we forget about character. But if we are true leaders we remember it is our privilege and responsibility to develop the character of our people. We must not disappoint them, but live and lead with character in all parts of our lives.

Credo by Theodore Roosevelt
President of the United States and Judo brown belt

It is neither the critic who counts, nor the man who points out how the strong man stumbled or the doer of deeds could have done better. The credit belongs to the man who is actually in the arena, whose face is marred by sweat and dust and blood; who errs and comes short again and again, who knows the great enthusiasms; the great devotions, and spends himself in worthy causes; who, at the best, knows in the end the triumph of high achievement and who, at worst, if he fails at least fails while daring greatly, so his place shall never be with those cold and timid souls who know neither victory or defeat.

Prologue

My grandfather's picture sits on my fireplace mantel. It shows a strong, handsome man in the prime of his life, frozen forever in black and white.

His name was John Thornbury. The first time he saw Nora Mae, she was sitting in a window watching the people pass by. She wore a light blue dress that didn't clash with her bright red hair. John pestered her friends for an introduction. Nora Mae was engaged to another man, but after one date with John, she quit the other fellow. They courted for 13 months, sitting on the front porch swing in the moonlight with the smell of roses all around.

They married in June 1936 and rented their first apartment, upstairs in an old Victorian house. On soft summer nights they would sleep on the balcony, wrapped up in their blankets and each other. Nora Mae had two girls, Cynthia and Karen. She buried a stillborn baby girl in the family cemetery and longed for more children.

John had a deep love for Nora Mae and the church. Like his father and grandfather before him, he became a minister. On Sundays, grandma Kitty would wave her arms above her head shouting praises to the Lord.

I often wondered if family tradition had pressured him into the ministry. I asked my Aunt Emma, in her 90's now, frail and translucent with age. She blinked with surprise, faded brown eyes widening. She said, "Why he was called, of course."

John was 36 when the cancer came. The family doctor gave him six months to live, then told them to go home and enjoy the time they had left. But Nora Mae, a small town Kentucky girl was determined to fight the cancer. She took John to New York City for surgery. He lived for three more years.

In the waning days of Johns' life, Nora Mae would give him a pain shot and sit by his bed, just the two of them, talking for hours about the happy times. John asked, "Promise me that you will remarry and have more children."

John Thornberry died at age 39. Nora Mae kept her promise. She remarried and had two more children.

I never knew my grandfather, but as I reached 36, I had the sense that time was running out, that my life was slipping through my fingers like water. I would wake at 3 a.m. in a blind panic, choking on fear, hearing as clearly as if God was in the room with me, "You don't have much time left."

I wasn't afraid to die. But I was desperately afraid that my life would not have mattered.

I began to question, what have I done that is important and lasting? What will I leave behind? Most of us are not remembered past two generations. We are immortalized only in our genes, like Nora Mae's bright red hair that skipped two generations and crowns the head of my little niece, Grace.

These questions kept me awake in the small hours before dawn. I would awaken from a deep sleep, my face wet with tears. I was being called, but to what?

I didn't tell anyone about my premonition. I put my house in order. I saw my pastor, drew up a will and established guardianship for my daughter. I made peace with my past.

I was watchful, waiting, more curious than fearful. My faith grew stronger. As a precaution, I went for a complete physical. A battery of tests found thyroid acceleration causing my heart to race, putting me at grave risk for a heart attack.

My subconscious had known there was a problem long before my body showed symptoms. Modern medicine slowed the urgency, but my restlessness remained.

When opportunity came in the form of downsizing, I felt incredibly light. I was free. I celebrated that new freedom with a two week European trip with my teenage daughter, our first vacation together.

Now I could do something bigger, something important and lasting, something that would make a difference in people's lives. What would it be?

Sometimes we get a second chance, disguised as a setback. A second chance to save our marriage, to rebuild relationships with our children. A second chance to breathe in vitality to a faltering career. I set out to answer my call.

Chapter One

An Argument For Character

What would it be like to live without fear? How would it feel to lead with honor? And what if you could look back at the end of your career without regret, knowing you had given your all?

These are times that test our courage. The nightly news is filled with revelations of accounting fraud, blind greed and staggering billion dollar equity losses that have destroyed our retirement dreams at home and impacted financial markets around the world. *The Wall Street Journal* and CNN's headlines are filled with stories of recession, bitter bear markets and massive downsizing. A corporate friend has survived job cuts of 40,000 employees. A small business owner told of waking at 3 a.m. every morning, gripped with anxiety. Would his company survive the recession?

These are times that test our character. A 2000 study by the Ethics Resource Center indicated that when times are the toughest, integrity matters the most. Companies in transition from mergers, acquisitions or restructuring are most at risk for unlawful or unethical behavior.[1] We know that when the stakes are high, it brings out the best and worst in human behavior.

I ran into an old friend, Emily, at a conference last fall. Her boss called as she changed planes in Chicago. "The company is laying off 16,000 employees next week," her boss said, "Choose which employees to cut." No one could have advance notice about the cutbacks.

Emily asked, "How can I make this decision without personnel files or my laptop?" Her boss, who operated from twin motivators of money and fear, offered to go through her organizational chart and draw X's through the boxes.

Emily did as she was asked; she struggled with her decision without the benefit of her administrative assistant, salary data, or performance reviews. Her staff was already lean, her people already working 12 and 14-hour days. Any cuts would further demoralize and overload them. Angry and upset at the effect on her people, she emailed her boss with several lay-off scenarios, outlining the trade-offs. Then, still in turmoil, she called her husband and asked his blessing.

Emily's next call was to her boss. She said, "Take me – take my VP job in place of these four employees." After that call, Emily was calm. She had peace. Emily left the company, trading off the security of a steady salary for a software startup. Her sacrifice resulted in one of her people being promoted, not as many were cut.

She didn't get a chance to say many goodbyes. But a week later, a big group from her former company took her to lunch.

Not surprisingly, Emily is being solicited by former employees who want to follow her to the software startup. They want a leader with character.

Winter 1996 – One burning question

"There is a difference between pain and injury."
Sensei

My interest in living and leading with character began with one burning question, is it possible for ordinary businessmen and women to lead with character? As an athlete I witnessed a great deal of courage and character in competition. But I was often disappointed in my corporate career.

Starting judo in January of 1996 took all of my courage. A confirmed couch potato for nearly twenty years, I was searching for an evening activity to do with my teenage daughter, Rachelle. Instead, I found my sport.

Judo is closer to Greco Roman wrestling than the better-known martial arts. An Olympic sport, Judo is full contact and combative (imagine football without helmets or padding), but does not involve kicking or striking techniques.

Instead, judo (Japanese for the gentle or yielding way) uses your opponent's strength and weight against him. A small person with a few weeks training can easily "flip" a larger person over his shoulder or hold him in a pin. Superior technique wins over strength and size. In competition, opponents start matches in a standing position, attempting to throw their opponent flat on their back, which immediately ends the match, like a knockout punch in boxing.

Judo throws combine breathtaking movement with grace and sheer athleticism. Grappling techniques seek submission through pins, chokes and arm locks. Judo requires peak cardiovascular conditioning for its five-minute, fast moving matches. Successful competitors have a firm grasp of the laws of physics and use strategy during matches, frequently called a chess game with bruises.

I began to practice judo, but I was not a natural athlete – instead, I was one of the club's worst students ever, in part because, six months earlier, a drunk driver had crossed the centerline, hitting my truck head on and wrenching my back.

Each time it was my turn to be thrown, I would tense up, adrenalin would flood my body, and I would tremble from head to foot. The fear of re-injuring my back was almost overpowering. Observing my struggle, the green belts took bets on how long I'd last.

Shelia Bunch, a brown belt, noticed my determination and became my practice partner. She was a heavy weight, solidly built, over 200 pounds of muscle, strong and fast, with explosive technique - all I wanted to be. Shelia spent extra time working with me, taking 30 falls each night, so I could learn how to throw.

In judo, just like life, you don't succeed solely on your own – your practice partners take falls to teach you to throw. I learned that the first rule of judo is to always protect your partner so she can come back to practice tomorrow. Judo is a sport of split second reactions. In competition, things happen so fast there is no time to think, just to react. With hundreds of hours of practice, muscle memory takes over.

Relying on dogged determination rather than any semblance of athletic ability, I trained hard, ending each practice with my heavy cotton uniform soaked with sweat, hair matted to my head, mascara making raccoon circles under my eyes.

Sensei (Japanese for teacher) had two rules. The first rule was to never surrender from a choke or a pin; to always keep fighting. Sensei said, "There is a difference between pain and injury. If you can withstand the pain and keep fighting, you may go on to win the match." I believed him. The second rule was no crying on the mat.

One night, assistant coach Clint Brizendine handed me a dog-eared packet of judo articles. The articles ragged with age and poorly copied, were 30 years old. I took them home and poured over the contents.

These writings went beyond the physicality of judo to philosophy. They spoke of the development of character in judo;

of living with courage, benevolence and character in all parts of your life.

I wasn't sure that philosophy had a place in modern sport. Curious, I began searching out writings on judo philosophy. My research led me back to judo's founder.

As a young Japanese in 1882, Dr. Jigoro Kano heard the echoes of the Samurai. He remembered the way of the warrior. Dr. Kano, a pacifist, modified the Samurai art of ju jitsu by changing or taking out dangerous techniques. He added a strict code of ethics and humanitarian philosophy, expecting his students to have outstanding character. Dr. Kano called his system of techniques and philosophy judo.

As judo spread throughout the Western world, it gained popularity as a sport and was included in World and Regional games, becoming an Olympic sport in 1964. The emphasis shifted from judo's intellectual and philosophical aspects to its physicality and athletic competition.

Still, the code of honor echoed through the sport. As I trained with and befriended athletes from Canada, France, Germany, Africa and New Zealand, the philosophy was always the same. It didn't matter if the principles hung on the walls of the practice center or were passed down orally from teacher to student; I found the same expectation of strong character.

As I began to compete, I realized that in the high stakes of sports I could discover a person's character very quickly. I could see things that might take me years to discover in a corporate setting. At every competition, I saw examples of courage and character. But my corporate life was different. I was often puzzled and disappointed by the shifting loyalties and lack of commitment. As the gap grew larger between my corporate and competitive life, I wondered if ordinary businessmen and women could lead with courage and honor.

I decided to find out. I spent two years conducting a literature review. I found a great deal written on the importance of business ethics, and many statistical studies on the benefits of organizational integrity, but very little on living and leading by a personal code of character.

I began interviewing a small circle of executives whom I had admired for years for their leadership and integrity. These are ordinary people living quiet lives, trying to make sense of our new business environment and hold fast to their principles. I was frequently surprised when prosaic leaders I had known professionally for years spoke with passion and eloquence.

I began to realize I had tapped into a hunger for meaning, for things left unsaid for many years.

As I conducted interviews in Paris in my fractured French and spoke to leaders in Canada and Europe, I discovered that though the legal framework for each country is different, core values are universal. These values cross cultural boundaries and transcend education and economic levels.

Each executive I interviewed referred me to others who had been their role models. In two years, I interviewed over 100 business leaders in North America and Europe. They shared their stories of success and failure. As I interviewed Olympians from my sport, they told me of years of sweat and sacrifice.

As I progressed with my interviews, themes rose to the surface, like holding up a mirror or listening to an echo of wisdom found in everyday leaders. I discovered that character begins with being crystal clear on your values that are grounded in the bedrock of your beliefs. People of character are not perfect – they juggle personal and professional roles and struggle to lead from the courage of their convictions. Character is strengthened through acts of integrity, loyalty and commitment that contain a measure of unselfishness and benevolence.

In studying the business leaders' and athletes' life lessons and hard won wisdom, I learned that by living and leading with character, you can make a great difference in your life, your children's lives and the lives of those you lead.

As I began speaking about character to professional groups, participants would come up after each presentation and say, "You are really talking about the Golden Rule. Or the Boy Scout Law. The teachings of Christ. Or Confucius."

They were right. These principles have remarkable similarities across cultures and classes. I realized that the analogy for learning was not as important as the application of the principles. I learned that people took what they needed from the presentations. Some needed encouragement. Some needed simple reinforcement. Others applied the principles to difficult decisions at work and at home.

As we struggled through a difficult year of corporate scandals, character took on a new resonance. But character these principles holds universal truths – long after Enron fades from the headlines, they will remain constant.

A wakeup call

"In places like New York, Chicago, and other notably tough turfs, people in every line of work were unfazed by evenings and weekends at the office, if that's what it took to land the big account or litigate the hot case. The rallying cry of the best and brightest was the big triple A: Ambition Above All. What a difference a year or two has made. Though ambition hasn't exactly skulked off the playing field, it seems to be taking on a more philosophical – possibly even chastened – form. As the bullish rush upward that characterized the Reagan romp is revealed to have been as destructive to companies as it was enriching to some individuals, the land of Milken honey has turned into a rubble-strewn landscape. Even those in the search-and-destroy brigade who never thought much beyond winning and who didn't worry a lot about the finer points of ethics are having second thoughts."
Owen Edwards, Upward Nobility

Substitute Clinton for Reagan, and Dot.com for Milken and Edward's words could have been written last week, not eleven years ago. Every decade or so, we go through cycles of economic boom and bust. In the early 1990s, the country was mired in recession and reeling from Wall Street insider trading scandals. Millions were out of work. Clinton ran and won the Presidency on the unofficial slogan, "It's the economy, stupid."

The recovery rocketed through eight years of growth and wealth building. Millions job-hopped and took the plunge into what seemed to be an unstoppable stock market buoyed by Dot.com companies.

In the spring of 2000, the bubble burst; first with the free fall of the Dot.coms, then our slowing economy was pushed into full-blown recession by the September 11th attacks and the Enron collapse. The party was officially over. Newly sobered and still grieving, we have pushed the pause button to re-examine our lives and priorities. What lessons can we learn? More importantly, what lessons can we apply?

This book, like any other, is a snapshot in time. It captures the mood of the country and measures our attitude toward business shaped largely by the twin elephants of 9/11 and Enron who stubbornly refused to leave the room during its writing.

"Winning" is written unapologetically for the baby boomers. Today, and for the next decade, we will enjoy peak positions of power and influence. But we, the boomers, the largest population land mass totaling 76.8 million, have squandered so many opportunities. We note, somewhat wistfully, that no one is calling us "The Greatest Generation." At least, not yet.

For many Americans, September 11th was a wakeup call, but wakeup calls can take many forms. I just received a phone call from a family friend whose wife is suddenly facing breast cancer. Her only warning came two weeks ago with sudden chest pain and an all-at-once visible lump. A battery of medical tests found the cancer on Thursday – surgeons plan to remove it on Monday. In the space of three days our friend's focus changed completely.

As many of us reach our 40s and 50s, we have caught a glimpse of our own mortality. Our peers are suddenly dropping with heart attacks and succumbing to cancer. Hospital visits remind us of the fragility of health. We have begun to ask the big questions.

Time passes and the trauma fades. We go on with our lives because we must. But we cannot shake the sense that we have been given a second chance.

In the introspection that has followed 9/11 and Enron, we have a window of opportunity – not just to clean up corporate corruption and restore faith in our financial markets, but to address the larger issues of how we live our lives and how we raise our children. A second chance to do something important and lasting; to pass down our life lessons and hard won wisdom. A second chance to live our legacy.

President John Fitzgerald Kennedy, who served 1,065 days in office, said in his inaugural address, "All this will not be finished in the first 100 days. Nor will it be finished in the first one thousand days, nor in the life of this administration, nor perhaps in our lifetime on this planet. But let us begin."[2]

In the aftermath of 9/11 and Enron, we have learned some painful lessons: life can be cut short. Careers can be uncertain. Wealth can quickly evaporate. But we can make a great difference. Let us begin.

A look back at business ethics

If we are to avoid another round of scandals in 2012, we must understand why business ethics failed corporate America. To understand where we must lead, we must first look back from whence we came.

The Harvard Business School was the first to offer a class on "social factors in business enterprise" in 1915, [3] but the modern business ethics movement grew out of widespread distrust of government after the Watergate scandal. Distrust with organizations spread with Ford Pinto's infamous exploding gas tanks and illegal payments overseas by government contractors.

In 1976, when Dr. Michael Hoffman, founder and Executive Director of Bentley College's Center for Business Ethics (CBE), first applied to the National Endowment for the Humanities for a grant to fund the center, he was rejected. The agency had never heard of business ethics.[4] When the *Wall Street Journal* first wrote about the CBE center, they called business ethics an oxymoron.[5]

Hoffman built CBE as a bridge between business and academia, encouraging networking between researchers and businessmen and linking the two worlds with practical and pragmatic application of theory. In the following decade, the need for CBE became clear.

The roaring 1980s were brought to an abrupt close by discovery of Wall Street insider trading and U.S. Department of Defense scandals surrounding $600 hammers and $800 toilet seats. The 1990s opened quietly except for a bond scandal at Solomon Brothers for illegal bidding at US Treasury auctions. Under the business-friendly climate of the Reagan-Bush era, business had an opportunity to police itself.

In 1991, the Federal Sentencing Guidelines for Organizations (FSGO) outlined corporate guidelines for an effective ethics program. By successfully following the guidelines, companies accused of criminal conduct can reduce federal fines by up to 95%. This is significant because, under stricter punishment guidelines for white-collar crimes, financial settlements can reach $500 million and more.

The FSGO outlined a minimum framework that includes, among other components: clear standards, ethics training for employees, a reporting system to report misconduct anonymously and establishing a track record of disciplining violators.[6]

For the first time, executives were held responsible for the misconduct of subordinates, but if organizations could show they made a serious, pro-active effort to prevent white-collar crime it would mitigate a judgment against the company and lessen their liability.

Organizations responded by creating ethics officer positions, installing ethics hotlines and drafting codes of conduct. The business of business ethics boomed, complete with training videos and consultants from the (former) Big Five accounting firms.

Companies realized their ethics programs went beyond lessening penalties and fines for employee misconduct – ethics were good public relations, helping to attract the best employees. Studies conducted by KPMG and the Ethics Resource Center show companies with high organizational integrity attract and retain good employees, increasing productivity and loyalty.[7]

In 1992, Dr. Hoffman helped form the Ethics Officer Association with 12 members. Today there are over 800 managers of ethics, compliance and business conduct programs.[8]

Top management is especially interested in organizational integrity because the stakes can become personally high. Individual members of the board can be held liable for misconduct and breached fiduciary duty. They can be, and have been, sued and sent to jail.

Ken Johnson, senior consultant of the Ethics Resource Center in Washington D.C., writes, "Liability, moreover is not limited to the organization alone. In a 1996 landmark decision, *In re Caremark International, Inc.,* the Delaware Court of Chancery warned that directors failing to assure that an organization takes adequate compliance measures can be held personally liable for subordinate wrongdoing."[9]

Is this fair? Tim C. Mazur, an ethics and compliance officer for Anthem, Inc., thinks so. "No one disputes that a board has the power to influence management behavior. Directors should use that power to influence company leaders to know and to care about integrity, values and compliance within the organization," argues Mazur. "And because the directors and officers of the company are in a position to prevent misconduct, they should be held personally liable."

Ten years after its inception, the carrot and stick combination of FSGO and director liability seemed to have worked. A 2000 study by the Society of Financial Service Professionals found that almost 90% of respondents reported that their companies have a written code of ethics and conduct.[10]

Enron was not supposed to happen.

What went wrong? Why wasn't FSGO enough?

The white-hot economy of the late 1990s put profits ahead of people. Business leaders were under tremendous pressure to do things they normally would not do to meet quarterly targets. Any miss in earnings per share by even a penny resulted in Wall Street's swift, sure punishment. CEOs were caught up in winning at all costs in a world where there was no black or white, only sophisticated shades of gray.

If we had been paying attention, we would have predicted that something like Enron was going to happen. In 2000 stories of accounting fraud and white collar crime became prevalent. *Fortune Magazine* found that "In 1999 and 2000 the SEC demanded 96 restatements of earnings or other financial statements – more than the past 9 years combined."[11]

Today, our headlines are filled weekly with corporate malfeasance and accessory accountants. You need only to pick up a morning paper or watch the nightly news for the discouraging evidence. We've almost become numbed, accepting the cost as part of our competitive business culture.

Yet, companies spend years and millions of advertising dollars building brand image and loyalty. Years of solid performance and profits can be wiped out overnight with one TV expose. When people make mistakes of judgment, the cost to companies is staggering. Litigation, plunging share prices and loss of market share directly affect the bottom line. There are unmeasured costs to damaged brand image and organizational good will. And there are human costs to morale and productivity - employees who lose heart as their company is dragged through the headlines.

But SEC investigations are slow, un-sexy reading. The scandal quickly fades from the headlines, replaced by the next company in hot water. Since 2000, some of the most golden names in business have been tarnished: Columbia HCA, Rite Aid, Sunbeam, Waste Management.

It took the Enron collapse - the second largest corporate bankruptcy in American history - to reach a "tipping point" of outrage over corporate criminality and greed.

The most egregious

The Enron story unfolded slowly to a country still consumed with grief after 9/11.

Enron, based in Houston, Texas, was ranked number seven on the Fortune 500, doing $100 billion of business in 2000. The stock market valued Enron at more than $63 billion.[12] Enron's growth was fueled by rising stock prices and Enron employees eagerly loaded up their 401(k) retirement plans with company stock.

On August 16, 2001, Enron executive, Sherron Watkins, warned of accounting problems. In a letter to Chairman Kenneth Lay, Watkins wrote, "I am incredibly nervous that we will implode in a wave of accounting scandals." Her letter was turned over to Enron's outside law firm, Vinson & Elkins, which investigated the charges and concluded that Watkins' concerns did not warrant a further widespread investigation.[13]

On October 16, 2001, in a conference call with Wall Street analysts, Lay disclosed that Enron had lost $618 million in the third quarter. It was soon revealed that the company had lost $1.2 billion in a labyrinth of partnerships that weren't counted on the company's books. These off-the-book partnerships enabled Enron to hide debts and boost the stock price, making it virtually impossible for outsiders to understand Enron's finances.[14]

On November 8, 2001, Enron issued a report saying that its numbers dating back to 1997 could no longer be relied on. Five years of profits had been grossly overstated and debts understated. By December 2, 2001, a mere six weeks later, the seventh largest company in terms of revenue in the United States had filed for bankruptcy.[15]

Many of Enron's 20,000 employees lost their 401(k) retirement savings when the company collapsed. About 5,000 lost their jobs.

The story quickly gained momentum with finger pointing and blame shifting between Enron and outside auditor, Arthur Andersen, which had been paid $52 million in 2000 for auditing and consulting services. At first, Andersen faced charges of incompetence for failing to ensure Enron's financial reports met the letter of accounting rules. But soon, incompetence charges gave way to accusations that Andersen allowed Enron to cook its books in exchange for lucrative consulting contracts.

By January of 2002, Enron and Andersen were claiming to have fired each other. When reports of document shredding at Andersen's Houston office surfaced, Andersen lost its reputation and most of its Fortune 500 clients.[16]   When Andersen was convicted of obstruction of justice for destroying documents in an effort to stop the SEC investigation, the Big Five became the Final Four.

The press searched for heroes and villains, cranking up the scandal apparatus in Washington D.C.   Stories of victimized investors and employees ran alongside tales of Enron's brutal company culture, Darwinian and politically vicious. In February of 2002 Enron's former vice chairman, Cliff Baxter was found slumped in his Mercedes, dead of a self-inflicted gunshot wound.[17]

For the first time accounting fraud became a national, not a business scandal. For the first time we realized white collar crime was not a victimless crime. The Enron story struck a chord because it showed there is a real cost to white-collar crime. Real people got hurt.

Thousands of shareholders watched their portfolio dwindle as Enron's $60 billion stock market valuation evaporated. Thousands more lost faith in our financial markets and the S&P began a protracted downward spiral.

We can count the stock market decline. But we cannot measure the fall-out from financial strain: the bankruptcies, divorces and illnesses brought on by stress. We cannot count the ruined careers and reputations damaged beyond repair.

Up to now, we've not had the stomach to send white-collar criminals to prison. Multi-million dollar civil fines have not stopped the production of products, everything from tobacco and defective tires to contaminated food, that kill people.

But as the drum beats calling for criminal prosecution grow louder, our outrage has indeed reached a tipping point. A headline in *Fortune Magazine,* hardly a hotbed of radicalism, screams, "It's time to stop coddling white-collar crooks. Send them to jail!"[18]

Why business ethics failed

We have learned that company codes of conduct don't prevent misconduct – even Enron had an ethics handbook. Up to this point, business ethics has been largely a legal issue because of the mandatory sentencing guidelines established in 1991 by the U.S. Sentencing Commission.

Company codes of conduct are often written in "legalese" by the legal or internal audit department. Drafted only to protect the organization from potential vulnerability; they poorly cover everything from discrimination to sexual harassment, from overseas bribery to insider trading.

Frequently, these codes of conduct are drafted without commitment from senior management or the involvement of those doing the work. This approach misses the opportunity to strengthen the company culture and reputation. A survey by Ethics Resource Center shows corporate ethics statements may actually lower morale if workers perceive them as nothing more than paper tigers.

Small to medium-sized businesses lack affordable ethics programs. "The Ethics Officer Association is the province of the Fortune 1,000. Those who can afford to have ethics programs can afford to have ethics officers," says ethicist Ken Johnson. "The ethics industry has not reached out to small and medium companies because it is not cost effective."

Organizational integrity programs offered by the (former) Big Five accounting firms (including Arthur Andersen) are too lengthy and expensive for small businesses.

But individual ethics consultants are viewed with suspicion by organizations. "The (former) Big Five accounting firms (organizational integrity programs) have an independent stamp of certainty and comfort," says ethicist Tim Mazur. "The business community is generally uncomfortable with ethicists. They are sometimes viewed with mistrust; as priests or tree huggers who want to return us to an agrarian society. Corporations are afraid an ethics cop will tell Proctor & Gamble to stop putting soapsuds in the water - or tell McDonalds not to kill cows to make hamburgers."

Business ethics failed corporate America because we allowed integrity to become a legal issue. We created thick codes of conduct that were as toothless as paper tigers and lost an opportunity to strengthen our company culture and turn rhetoric into reality.

But if the Ethics Officer Association is exclusive to Fortune 1,000 companies and ethics statements and codes of conduct don't go far enough, what should we do?

It always comes down to the individual who has to make the right decision. "One must integrate individual and organizational integrity," argues Dr. Hoffman, "Because good people can be brought down by bad organizations. Integrity is not just the individual, it is reciprocal."

Today many companies have learned that organizational integrity is more than following laws and regulations. They are evolving from reactive, post-scandal compliance programs to pro-active values leadership.

"Today there is pressure put on people to meet targets, pressuring them into things they normally wouldn't do," concludes Hoffman. "It takes courage and moral character to stand up to pressure. It takes ordinary people with good habits of character."

Individual integrity

"It has become fashionable to demonize corporations and corporate managers...that is an incorrect perception promulgated by the media. Of course, there are some bad apples, but managers and executives are real people with real families, real values and real hopes for the future of their children. They are doing a very difficult job with virtually no public support or understanding."
Heber MacWilliams

A year filled with screaming headlines of corporate scandals has taken a heavy toll in corporate confidence and sent stock prices spiraling downward. Even innocent business leaders have been painted with the broad brush of suspicion.

Most CEOs have kept their silence, concerned that bookkeeping errors might be mistaken for accounting fraud. Many are baffled by a dizzying array of new regulations and paralyzed by indecision as they try to lead in a volatile business environment. It is time to break the silence and restore public confidence in our corporate leadership.

Today, CEOs are under intense pressure to certify financial results and guarantee the integrity of the organizations they lead. But CEOs can't do it alone – anyone who has managed a large department knows it is impossible to know everything subordinates say and do. The responsibility for integrity must rest on the shoulders of every business leader.

If you believe, as I do, that corporate corruption is a few bad apples and not the whole rotten barrel, it is up to us to correct this crises. We have a responsibility to reach out to tomorrow's leaders, to re-enforce in them the will to do what is right.

If you are tired of the trivial and trendy and business fads; if you are weary of buzzwords and superficial fixes to deep-rooted problems, then you will agree it is time to return to the fundamentals. Too often we become infatuated with the new when we need to firm up our foundation. Though it seems out of step with our sophisticated society, we are hearing new calls for an old fashioned, outmoded concept – character in leadership.

Business fads blaze hot and fade fast. They fail us because they distract from true leadership. Character in leadership is not a buzzword; rather it keeps you grounded in a solid core of values when life snaps into fast forward.

Instead of looking outward for answers, we need to look inward to leadership fundamentals that are deeply embedded and almost forgotten. We must step into the leaderless void and learn to speak a common language centered on core values and create a covenant of character.

The blinding white light of getting rich quick caused many in business to lose their way. The way back to the fundamentals has been worn by the 100 business leaders who shared their experience – leaders who have made mistakes and fallen short – and who have gotten back up. The knocked down signposts showing the way back to the fundamentals have been righted in the following chapters:

- The power of integrating personal and professional values.
- Moving beyond the worn out clichés of balance to benevolence.
- Leading from the courage of your convictions.
- Making a lasting contribution.
- Recapturing loyalty and restoring trust.
- Living and leading with character.
- Living your legacy.

Enron and 9/11 took us beyond business ethics to issues of how we live our whole lives.

Let us begin.

Chapter One

Leadership Questions

- Can character be taught? Or is it too late by the time a person joins your organization?

- Can one person make a difference in an organization?

- Can you give me an example of character from your own experience or what you have observed?

- What character challenges are common to your profession?

- What would you do if you had a talented but unethical person in your department?

- What went wrong at Enron? Why didn't more employees protest unethical behavior?

- How can business leaders make their ethics statement a living, breathing commitment?

- How can business leaders model character-centered leadership?

Chapter Two

Bridging The Values Generational Gap

"Children without values are like a coatroom without hooks."
George Gecowets

In judo, the teacher, or sensei plays an important role in the development of his student's character. Keeping a commitment to practice three times a week, 52 weeks a year teaches students perseverance, making them stronger mentally and physically. Competition builds their courage. Character comes from accepting wins and losses with equal measures of humility and grace. Judo goes beyond teaching physical technique to teaching the values of courage, character and benevolence.

Most of us learn our values at home. Our parents teach us right from wrong, though sometimes our grandparents or an exceptional teacher makes an impact. Often it wasn't so much what our parents said but what they did day-in and day-out. "It is inescapable that parents shape your values by their lifestyle and little day-by-day events. I remember how hard my Dad worked, and how exhausted he was at the end of the day. It wasn't anything he said, but I learned that you owe your employer a day's work for a day's pay," says consultant, Cyndy Karon.

These childhood values become more important as we age. We are hungry for re-enforcement of the values we were raised on, the lessons learned from our parents, churches and schools. We've reached a point of success where we pause to catch our breath and measure the cost of the long climb. By the time we reach midlife, many of us have been knocked down. We may have faced failure in our career or marriage - we may have survived a serious illness or loss of a parent.

As we grow older and have a greater sense of self, our values become seamless. These values become integrated in all you do and carry into all parts of your life. Our parent's generation searched for answers in their churches, civic groups and families. But today, with our families scattered across the country and repeated relocation resulting in isolation from our communities; work has become the main connector in our search for values.

Why values?

"People desperately need to know that what they do makes a difference in the organization's success."
Heber MacWilliams

Today there is a movement sweeping corporate America, a return to the importance of values and character in leadership. Businesses' growing interest in values is not altogether altruistic. It is driven by an authentic need to attract and use the talents of a shrinking and increasingly independent workforce.

Company values give a sense of purpose that goes beyond profit making. People come to the office with more than their bodies and minds. They are searching for meaning and purpose in their lives and their work. We want to feel that what we do all day has a positive impact on our lives and our communities, that we are making some small difference in the world. We want to belong to a workplace where people share a sense of purpose beyond making money. We long to connect our idealism with what we do at the office.

Of course we work to pay the mortgage and save for our children's college tuition. We labor to make the car payments, put braces on our kid's teeth and food on the table. But people want more than a paycheck. In exchange for the long hours we spend at the office, we want our work to be a source of satisfaction. We want to feel we are of service to something larger than ourselves; to dedicate ourselves to work that makes a difference.

For many companies, the effort to create meaning at work grew out of repercussions of "rightsizing" which resulted in a dispirited and disloyal workforce. Some believe values leadership is one more program catering to the concerns of baby boomers. But the boomers are not the only ones looking for meaningful work; the search for purpose is even more pronounced for Generation X.

Hard-bitten business veterans place values leadership squarely into human resources "warm fuzzies" training. "Values based leadership training is like standing before a group with a plate of cookies and asking, would you like one?" says trainer, Ted Fancher. But in the ongoing war for talent, values can become a powerful tool for recruitment and retention. Company values can provide a common ground, a foundation on which to work towards a shared purpose.

Employees come into your organization with their values largely shaped, but companies can benefit by communicating their values and connecting them to leadership. For Gen X, work may be the only place they get values training.

In an early 1990's Home Depot employee orientation video, Bernie Marcus looks squarely at the camera and says, "We take care of our own." During my three-month orientation with Depot, I traveled non-stop from store to store. Everywhere I went, the associates told me, "This is the greatest company in America. I never want to work anywhere else." Their energy and excitement was contagious. In those days, I would have paid the company for the privilege of being a part of it.

Company values are passed down orally because people learn through stories and bond through a shared history. Ken Langone,

Lead Director for The Home Depot, used to tell the story of an hourly associate who won the lottery. An overnight millionaire, he still worked every day, loving the company more than money.

As leaders, we must live by those values - not merely mouthing the words but living and breathing them in our daily actions. One month after joining Depot, Jimmy Ardell sat with me in a hotel lobby in New Jersey. "It is your responsibility to carry on the culture," he said. "Me? I just started," I responded. But Jimmy was right. It is our responsibility as leaders to perpetuate the culture and values of the organization, to share the standards we live by.

In a period of high growth and change, it can be hard to preserve company values and culture. Over time, and with an influx of new employees, company values can be lost. When a company fails to recruit people who share its values or can become indoctrinated into the culture, a good culture can be corrupted. One person can destroy a department. However, if a company is committed to its values, it will seek out people who share those values.

The Harvard Business School asked over 800 MBAs and executives what our future business leaders should be taught. By a wide margin, the most frequent answer was morals, values and ethics. Many would argue that values must be taught in the home; that developing character is the responsibility of parents, pastors and teachers. The cynics would say it is too late to teach adults right from wrong.

"Can ethics be taught?" is the question Dr. Hoffman of CBE has spent his 25-year career trying to answer.

In his book, *Ethics Matters*, Hoffman writes, "Too many employees are not receiving any grounding in values from their home, their church, their school or their community." He argues that, like it or not, corporate America has taken on the job of teaching values to its people, a sociological sea change that is as widespread as it is necessary.

Corporate America is uncomfortable assuming this responsibility, but employees are not entering organizations firmly grounded in their values. A 2000 KPMG study showed that 76 % of employees have observed unlawful or unethical conduct on the job.[1]

Four generations apart

"Generation X is entering more turbulent waters than our generation faced. They must be prepared to contribute and to serve."
Fred Ball

As leaders we face the challenge of connecting company values to a diverse workforce. To attract, retain and motivate four very different generations of workers, we must understand their unique perspectives and the national events that shaped their values. To maximize performance, the four generations need to work together in harmony, bridging the generational divide through shared values.

The "Matures" generation, totaling 61.8 million, were born between 1909 and 1945. They lived through the Great Depression, World War II and the Cold War. Most of them grew up poor and were lifted to post war prosperity by The New Deal and the GI Bill of Rights. We boomers grew up hearing austerity stories from our Depression era parents.

When we were younger, we called them the "old guard," resenting them for standing between us and changing the world. Now we appreciate their work ethic, reliability and company loyalty. We, the boomers, along with the Matures, have, for better or worse, created the workplace of today.

Matures value commitment, shared sacrifice, financial and social conservatism. They respect authority and believe in working their way to the top.[2] They worked hard to pay the bills and put food on the table. They felt fortunate to have jobs, especially if they had a good job that could send us to college and on to a better life.

The boomer generation faces different challenges and expectations. We face tremendous pressure to achieve. We want to be successful and rack up all the prizes: the big house, the luxury car, the 401(k) war chest. And in this race to succeed, some of us have lost our values along the way.

The Boomers

"I often think about what my father would have said if he had lived to see my success."
John Thomas Mentzer

My generation, the baby boomers, were born from 1946 to 1964. The baby boom began in 1946 when the World War II veterans came home and lasted until 1964, when the birth rate began to decline.[3] N.A. Barnett, for example, contributed to the postwar population increase. When he came home from serving in World War II in 1946, he and wife Therese had seven children in ten years.

There are 76.8 million baby boomers; an enormous population bulge which is still being digested. We continue to transform all elements of society. We competed fiercely at every life stage - in the classroom for grades, for our first jobs and every rung up the corporate ladder. As a generation, we boomers value idealism, individualism and self-improvement. We are largely defined by our work and our endless quest for self-actualization.

Because the baby boom generation spans so many birth years, it can be difficult to point to a defining moment. Boomers attitudes are influenced by where they were born on the time continuum between '46 and '64 and their age during the national events that shaped our country - Vietnam, the Civil Rights movement, John F. Kennedy's assassination and Watergate. Their birth date (the Vietnam draft ended in 1972) helped to determine if they became a hippie, served in Vietnam or dodged the draft. Those born after 1960 missed most of the defining moments all together and came of age in the vacuity of the mid 1970s and consumerism of the roaring 1980s.

I was born in 1961, toward the tail end of the baby boom. I grew up in a country eager to be carefree, to put the bitterness and division of Vietnam behind.

The youngest of my generation are just now hitting their stride, turning 36 this year. They are at their peak earning, power and parenting years. At age 56, the oldest of the boomers are, shockingly, entering their pre-retirement years. Boomers in the middle are facing empty nests and issues of maturation and mortality.

Gen X

"Saying 'whatever' is a malaise."
Heber MacWilliams

It is Generation X, born 1965-1978 with a population of only 52.4 million[4] that gives the boomers the most headaches. They are certainly the most criticized generation. The boomers complain that Gen Xers have no work ethic, are disloyal and self-centered. We gripe that they expect to rocket to the top, to enjoy all the perks of power, money and prestige without paying their dues. We whine that they don't respect their elders - then clap our hands over our mouths, amazed that we sound just like our parents – amazed that we have become someone's elders. We smugly predict Gen X will morph into our boomer likeness once saddled with mortgages and family obligations, just as the hippies turned yuppies in the 1980s.

The dichotomy of Gen Y

"We baby boomers basically destroyed the world. We created latchkey kids, urban deterioration, crack and downsizing; and we polluted the water and air. We were just about consumption. Gen Y comes along and says, "Wait a second, I've got to fix some of this."
Patrick Adams, quoted in Credit Union Management

It is too early to tell how Gen Y, sometimes called the echo boomers, will turn out. Born between 1979 and 2001 with 77.6 million members; the first wave is just now entering the workforce. Early reports are hopeful – Gen Y values neo-traditionalism, technological adeptness and a compartmentalized work and life.[5]

A recent study showed that Gen Y workers are more dutiful and dedicated than Gen Xers, expressing loyalty and strong values systems.[6]

Gen Y is an oddly divided generation – large numbers protest globalization and the International Monetary Fund while equally large numbers compete fiercely for admission to top Ivy League schools.

Of course, people don't fall into tidy categories. They refuse to be neatly defined and packaged by the media. Rather, the generations overlap. Even a few years difference in birth date affects perceptions. Attitudes wash over from one generation to the next.

Understanding Gen X

"Generation X is wearing me out. Their values are warped from growing up with no parents in the home. They wreak havoc in the organization."
Harriet Seward

The combination of maturing boomers, soon to start retiring and the significantly smaller Gen X presents a dramatically shrinking workforce. When the economy improves, the talent wars will continue for many years.

Because there are so few of them, our challenge as leaders is to understand and accommodate Gen X'ers. The Bureau of Labor Statistics projects that the number of people in the labor force between the ages of 25 and 44 will decrease by 3.7 million between 1998 and 2008. By contrast between 1978 and 1988, the same age group in the labor force increased by 10.7 million.

The *Harvard Management Update* predicts that U.S. labor markets will remain relatively tight for the next 20 years. To recruit and retain the best of Gen X we must speak to and support their values. To understand Gen X we need to begin by looking in the mirror.

Our generation (boomers) came of age in the "greed is good" mentality of the roaring 80s. We had to have it all and have it at once. If we weren't happy, it was easy to change jobs, change spouses, and change our lives. In those self-centered times we raised a generation of children on television and divorce. On Sundays, we were too worn out from work to take them to church. Now they are grown up and entering the workforce. No one has taught them values.

Why Gen X doesn't want to be boomers

"There is a transition and some resentment going on today between the old and new generations. The baby boomers are moving into pre-retirement. We try to share our experience with Gen X, but it falls on deaf ears."
Ted Fancher

When I guest lecture at Western Kentucky University, I tell the college students how the boomers perceive them. I recite the litany of stereotypical complaints: Gen X lacks ambition and loyalty, they choose recreation over carving out a career, they have a low work ethic, they won't commit. "The first time a Gen X worker didn't show up, we drove up and down the highway, thinking they had been in an accident," I tell them, "Gen Xers will simply abandon a job and never call to let you know they're not lying dead in a ditch."

But when I listen to Gen X perceptions of the boomers, it is equally unflattering. They don't want to grow up to be like us. They don't want to repeat our mistakes.

Our generation believed that our family's happiness came from financial security. Success was defined as rising through the ranks and grabbing the brass ring. We believed we were being good providers for our children by working endless hours and weekends, by foregoing vacations. We thought company loyalty would benefit our family so we agreed to relocate frequently and make sacrifices to keep our feet firmly planted on the corporate ladder. But the recession of the early 1990s wiped out entire layers of management. Our children watched and realized we had kept an unfair bargain.

They don't want to grow up to be like us, and they don't want their kids to grow up without parenting. Many of Gen X grew up as latchkey kids with divorced, workaholic parents. Television's surrealistic programming substituted for solid parenting. This lack of parental involvement produced a generation that is cynical, independent and self-sufficient. "I don't want my child raised by television," one young man said firmly.

The first wave of Gen X college graduates entered the workforce in the recession of the early 1990s when downsizing, lay-offs and staff reductions first became common. Many saw their parents and older colleagues lose their jobs after years of loyal service, leaving them skeptical and disloyal toward organizations.[7]

These young adults watched us struggle through job anxiety and failure. "It is better to work for myself," the students tell me. "Better to call my own shots, to live where I want to live, and to work only to make a living."

Recently, I wrote an article for *Entrepreneur* magazine on the courage it takes to remain an entrepreneur in our difficult economy. The magazine guidelines dictated that my interview subjects had to be less than 35 years of age. I panicked – how would I find these young entrepreneurs? I sent out about a dozen emails requesting interview leads.

Within a week I was flooded with interview subjects – young, smart and successful, all in their early 30s. I found that Gen X has a strong entrepreneurial spirit. Today, twenty-five percent of small businesses are headed by entrepreneurs under 34.[8]

I didn't start my business until I was 39 – by the time I finished my interviews with bright, successful, ambitious young entrepreneurs I was the one who felt like a slacker!

Gen X – working to live

"For my son's generation, the job is a means to an end. They achieve goals outside of work. My son dropped out of Georgia Tech to valet park. For him, the job is a necessity to get the money to do what he wants. That is a waste of a good mind. But maybe when we re-evaluate our own lives, maybe we're the ones who are wrong. Maybe they have it right."
Talley Jones

Gen Xers are unwilling to sacrifice life and family for a career. They are not willing to climb the corporate ladder when they feel the rungs are crumbling. They work to live, not live to work, valuing leisure time, recreation and family above career success, promotions or transfers.[9] A study by Gross and Scott found that Gen Xers see little value in material possessions for which their parents worked, preferring to spend more time with friends and family. They would prefer to finish in second place if it meant having more time for recreation, travel and non-career goals.[10]

This generation has a strong desire to balance work and life for a better quality of life. They will push for a compressed workweek, flextime, telecommuting, leaves and sabbaticals to juggle family responsibilities.

A September 2001 study, by Catalyst, of 1,300 Gen X professionals asked which of the following values and goals were extremely important.[11] The results:

To have a loving family.	84%
To enjoy life.	79%
To obtain and share companionship with family and friends.	72%
To establish a relationship with a significant other.	72%
To have a variety of responsibilities.	22%
To earn a great deal of money.	21%
To become an influential leader.	16%
To become well known	6%

The same study, taken ten or fifteen years earlier with boomers, would have shown far different priorities. If we are to bridge this generation values gap we must understand and respect Gen Xers' values.

Making the hard choices

"I try to preach to Gen X and Y to put in the effort, make a contribution and be a team player. People have to respect you – you can't force your way up the ladder. It's effort, contribution and teamwork – and then patience."
Tim Barber

After years of talking to hundreds of college students, I believe Gen X will rewrite the rules for business and redefine success on their own terms. I am hopeful that they will be better parents than our generation.

Recently I asked an evening class of business students, all bright and ambitious, all working full time and taking night classes, to make a hard choice. Would they rather work for Company A, making less money but living a fuller life with family and friends or choose an accelerated career with Company B? With one exception, the students chose Company A. I had to stop them from pouncing on the one student who chose Company B. The students justified their choice with stories of their parent's downsizing and absentee parenting.

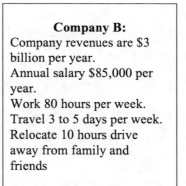

Company A:	Company B:
Company revenues are $600,000 per year.	Company revenues are $3 billion per year.
Annual salary $45,000 per year.	Annual salary $85,000 per year.
Work 50 hours per week.	Work 80 hours per week.
No travel.	Travel 3 to 5 days per week.
Live close to family.	Relocate 10 hours drive away from family and friends
Close friendships	

If we can look beyond our own generational blinders to understand what drives Gen X behavior, designing a retention program is not that different from any other generation.

Gen X demands interesting work and needs daily praise and recognition. Since they don't believe in climbing the ladder, they want to make a difference from day one. We must give them a tool kit of skills, offer up-to-date training to make them more marketable during the next downturn. We must tap into their talents and give them timely and constructive feedback, including our expectations for a strong, consistent work ethic. This doesn't mean the boomers should pander to Gen Xers' every passing fancy. It does mean treating them with less exasperation and more recognition that we don't have all of the answers. Boomer leaders sometimes become surrogate parents for Gen X – they respond by becoming remarkably loyal to the leader but not to the company.

To attract and keep the best, regardless of their generation, we must support their values. It is their energy and commitment that gives your company a competitive edge. When people become clear in their values, they search for a company that matches their values. As a leader you must help your people clarify their values.

By understanding their priorities, they'll become more decisive, confident and responsible. And unless they are clear about their personal values, they'll have no way of judging if the corporate values agree with their own.

Can one person make a difference?

"Yes, if you're in the right organization that values integrity. If not, you're nothing but a nuisance."
Harriet Seward

"But wait," you argue, "I am just one person. I can't change the company." But you can change you. You can change your department. Every organization is made up of a mosaic of departments, each with its own culture and storehouse of stories, each working toward achieving the organization's overarching objectives. The people you lead know your values. They see you day in and day out, handling details and making split second decisions. They will forgive your small failings.

One person can make a difference. The level and impact of difference is dependent on the leadership position. The CEO is responsible for setting the values and vision of the organization. But you can build a departmental culture based on values by telling your people what the organization stands for, what it is trying to achieve and what is in it for them. Begin by becoming crystal clear on who you are, what you believe and what you value.

Drilling to the bedrock of your beliefs

"Leading from your personal values is hard - you are on display all the time."
Ted Fancher

In *Built to Last*, authors Collins and Porras start out by shattering a dozen common myths of great companies.

They contend "the crucial variable is not the content of a company's ideology but how deeply it believes its ideology and how consistently it lives, breathes and expresses it in all that it does." Visionary companies do not ask, "What should we value?"

They ask, "What do we actually value deep down to our toes?" Isn't it just as important to figure this out for our own lives?

Begin by asking who you are and what you stand for. Determine your core values – your guiding set of principles that will not be compromised. Ask yourself, "Am I living my life congruent with my core values? Am I missing something important in my life? Am I raising my children right and passing down my values? What matters most?"

Give yourself quiet time to think through your values and write your responses. It doesn't matter if you write in a fancy journal or jot your notes on a yellow legal pad.

What does matter is doing more than simply think about your answers. Take the time to write down your answers. Put your journal away for a week, then come back to re-read and revise your answers. The process will help you determine the bedrock of your beliefs.

Partial list of core values:

Accomplishment	Achievement	Admiration	Adventure
Advocacy	Ambition	Authority	Beauty
Business	Career	Challenge	Competition
Country	Culture	Discipline	Drama
Duty	Education	Enjoyment	Environment
Equality	Excitement	Exercise	Experience
Faith	Family	Freedom	Fun
God's Will	Good Income	Happiness	Health
Home	Honor	Hope	Humor
Independence	Income	Influence	Integrity
Intellect	Involvement	Joy	Leadership
Leisure	Love	Loyalty	Mastery
Materialism	Maturity	Military	Morality
Nonconformity	Obedience	Ownership	Patience
Persistence	Play	Power	Professionalism
Rebellion	Recognition	Religion	Responsibility
Rewards	Riches	Satisfaction	Self-reliance
Sincerity	Spirituality	Success	Survival
Teamwork	Tradition	Truth	Well-being
Winning	Wisdom		

Once you are clear on your own values and purpose, how do you keep from checking your values at the door at work? How can you live your values and the company's values in harmony?

Write down the company's values in your own words. Compare your personal values and the company values. How closely do they match-up? Can you buy into the company values? Can you put your values into practice at work? Can you connect your personal values to the company purpose, core values and mission?

The next step in determining a match between your personal and company values is to read aloud your company mission statement. What does the company mission statement mean to you? Don't just parrot the words (they are likely written in consultant speak) but rewrite it in your own words.

Dust off your personal mission statement from the management retreats in the 1990s. Boil it down to one sentence in the plainest language you can muster. Your personal mission statement should state: this is what I believe in, this is what I am committed to improving, and this what I love with my whole heart.

Your personal mission statement should be memorable enough to quote. It should reflect you at your best, be a vision for your life that is motivating, and give guidance during change. My mission statement has guided my decisions and set my priorities for a dozen years. It reads, "Achieving a balance between career, family and community to leave a lasting contribution."

If you can't find your mission statement or discover that it is hopelessly out of step with your life, re-read any of Stephen Covey's books from the early 90's. Sometimes we become infatuated with the latest business fad when what we need is to return to the fundamentals.

Character-centered leadership is not a panacea or an easy answer to today's challenges. But your leadership must be grounded in your beliefs as you make decisions about people and strategy. Your values become bedrock in a storm of uncertainty and change. Today we cannot predict where we are going or how our lives will unfold, but we can understand who we are and what we believe.

A larger issue of leadership and character

"The leaders talked about the importance of values at work, but their private life was deplorable. One cannot have values in the office and a sham in private life. You cannot turn integrity on and off – it must carry over to all that you do."
Bernie Hale

I would argue that above the mundane daily details of getting the job done, of meeting quarterly and annual performance goals, there is a larger issue of leadership and character. How you live your life at work and at home makes a difference because how you lead influences the people who work for you. It affects the kind of leaders they will become.

When I graduated from The Ohio State University, my first job was as a regional transportation manager for The Limited. In those days – the late 1980s - The Limited was famous not only for its fashion, but also for the speed with which it distributed products to its stores. When fashion is as perishable as lettuce, speed and getting there first is critical.

The distribution system had been designed by one of The Limited's original founders. My job was to review the transportation network; find cost and service efficiencies, and put it back together. This was heady stuff for a new college graduate. I was full of myself, intoxicated with the power.

One day, Steve, an older and wiser friend, took me to lunch. As we ate, we talked about my exciting new job. He asked me if I would like to see the impact of all my changes on The Limited. "Sure," I replied. He put his finger in my glass of water.

"Any time you think you're indispensable, remember this," he said, "When you work in a big organization, you're making quite an impression on it. There is no doubt. When you leave, here's what happens." Steve took his finger out of my water. "That is the long term effect you will have," he said. The water stood still.

Of course now I couldn't drink the water. Then he told me something that made me lose my appetite. "The impact you will have at The Limited and in your career is scarcely a ripple," he said. "The only lasting impact you will have is on the people you lead."

In my logistics career, I managed budgets worth hundreds of millions of dollars. I built vast transportation networks. But the only lasting things of value are the men and women I mentored and their leadership in corporate America today. Your legacy is what you are living today. It is the leadership affect you have on the people around you.

It seems appropriate to give a Gen Xer the final word. "My generation's career goals are not necessarily to rise within the company or to make the most money as has been the goal of previous generations. Rather we have a goal to retire at a young age," says Timothy Davis, 27. "Although we grew up living in expensive homes and riding in nice cars, most of my co-workers appear satisfied driving used cars and purchasing smaller homes. They take pride in the fact that they are making large contributions to their 401(k) plans. I see young professionals working long hours, but they do it with an ending point in mind rather than with hopes for a promotion. It is almost like we see our career as a band-aide and the quicker we pull it off, the less painful it will be."

Chapter Two

Leadership Questions

- Who shaped your values growing up? Who was your role model?

- Who has been your most influential boss – why?

- Which five values are most important to your organization?

- How do your professional values differ from your personal values?

- Is it the company's responsibility to teach values?

- Do you consider yourself to be a role model?

- How do you motivate the new generation?

- What values will you pass on to the people you lead?

- How have your values helped you in life?

Winning The Balance Tug of War

Fall 1996

After nine months of judo, I was in peak physical condition, easily making my competition weight. I was lean, fit and muscular for the first time in my adult life.

I felt strong and had boundless energy, coming home to run three miles after each judo practice. My mother, however, was concerned as thyroid problems run rampant through our family.

On a muggy Friday afternoon before the Labor Day weekend, the specialist read my thyroid test results and outlined treatment options. He warned that an overactive thyroid was causing my heart to race, putting me in immediate danger of cardiac arrest. I had the holiday weekend to decide on immediate surgery to remove my thyroid or radiation to destroy it. The specialist was brusque with the risks and long-term side effects of treatment. When he told me I could never have another child, I felt as if my body had betrayed me. Suddenly my strength seemed like a mockery. I left his office in tears.

When I got home, I called my mother, sobbing into the phone for maternal comfort. I asked, "Am I being punished?"

Punished, I thought, for all the years of me first, my career, the travel and the workaholic weeks. I had lived my life as though there would be plenty of time later. Later, when my marriage was stronger. Later, when my career slowed. Later, when I didn't travel so much. There was going to be time later, to have another baby. But time had run out.

I thought, if God is grieving with me, if He is weeping with me over this great loss, I can bear it. But if God is turning his face from me, I cannot bear it. I cannot.

In the months that followed, I began treatment to slow my thyroid. In the cold darkness of Kentucky's long winter nights, I grieved quietly and deeply over my lost child. My arms felt empty, as if a child had been snatched away. Every place I went, there were babies. They smiled at me from strollers, flirted with me over their parent's shoulders. My heart ached – my arms were empty.

I started coming to judo an hour early to watch the children's practice. Sensei invited me to bow onto the mat to keep order with a dozen energetic kids. A tiny girl with dark brown hair and almond shaped eyes tagged along with her older brother to practice. She was too young at age three to start judo, but she sat in my lap and watched practice. Rachel was a girly girl, proud of her new dress covered with flowers and dancing ponies. She pointed out her hair barrettes and pink fingernail polish for our admiration.

Rachel crawled into my lap every practice and wrapped her arms around my neck. She loved me and needed me, even if it was only two nights a week. She had lost her Mother and I had lost my chance for a second child. As the months passed, our hearts healed.

As the years went by, I became involved with the other children. Our junior judo team grew in size and skill, winning three state championships. I became coach Rebecca. Today I train the junior team three days a week, 52 weeks a year. We travel and compete around the country. I'm there to watch their confidence and skills grow, to rejoice in the wins and commiserate in the losses. Now when people ask me if I have children, I say, "Yes, I have 30." And my arms are full.

When the cost is too high

From the time I was 13, I had a clear vision of my future: riding on a plane, wearing a navy blue suit, briefcase tucked at my feet. I would travel somewhere far away from the fields of corn of my childhood.

Many women of my generation shared that dream and made it a reality. But at what price? My friend called to tell me of her new job, a top spot at a Fortune 100 company. But her voice was sad – as she started her new job, her marriage had ended. She and her husband had moved four times in four years to accelerate their careers. Four years of rapid relocations, long hours and being a trailing spouse had put too great a strain on their young marriage.

Time Magazine's April 15, 2002 cover story, "Making time for a baby," told of women who had worked too hard, traveled too much and waited too long. Economist Sylvia Ann Hewlett's national survey of 1,647 high achieving women in corporate America found that 42% were still childless after age 40. 49% of women who earned over $100,000 were childless.[1] Recent Census data showed that childlessness has doubled in the past 20 years – 1 in 5 women between ages 40 and 44 is childless.[2]

Putting aside all of the arguments about an anti-feminist agenda, and questions about priorities and policies, the biological clock doesn't lie. Despite the miracle baby headlines, a 42 year-old woman's chance of having a baby using her own eggs is less than 10%. For these women, time had run out, making childlessness a "creeping non-choice."[3]

Thousands of career women try for years to have a baby and grieve in private. Too late, they realize the cost is more than they had calculated, but we cannot turn back the clock, we cannot get that time back.

Women are not the only ones who have paid too high a price.

My interviews found men who told cautionary tales of families lost through divorce, of devoting their entire life to building a company, to having a life without meaning after they were downsized. Men who could barely bring themselves to speak of years lost from their children's lives. Bob's story is shared by several.

"I broke my finger reaching for the brass ring," says Bob Vines. His story starts with a love affair with a company. He continues, "It was hard not to fall in love with IBM. One of IBM's three fundamental principles was respect for the individual. They practiced that principle in every company action. Employees were trusted implicitly. And, most importantly, employment was guaranteed as long as you did your job. The company had never laid off an employee in its entire history."

With this special treatment of employees, however, came some "special" expectations. On Bob's second Monday on the job, as he sat down at his desk, a peer looked over and said, "We missed you on Saturday."

Bob thought, "Am I expected to work on Saturdays?" At any of his other jobs he would have expected overtime pay or at least compensatory time for working weekends. The next Saturday, Bob worked. In fact, he almost always worked Saturdays. He didn't mind because the job was so much fun, and the people were great. Bob loved IBM. And IBM surely loved him back—by his third year with the company, Bob had reached the third level of management. Hundreds of people reported to him.

Not long ago, Bob was down in his basement cleaning up and rearranging boxes. When he picked up a box, a photograph popped out and dropped onto the floor. A little girl of five or six, missing many of her baby teeth, smiled up at him. Bob held the picture up to his wife and asked, "Who is this?"

"What do you mean?" she answered. He repeated, "Who is this?" She replied, incredulously, "You mean, you don't recognize your own daughter?" Bob didn't say anything else. His wife went back upstairs but he stood looking at the photo, trying to remember. When his daughter was six years old that was probably the year that IBM first introduced the Pro printer, or maybe it was the second Pro printer, or maybe the third. That was a busy time! Bob didn't take any vacation that year. He could even remember working Christmas Day. Bob's picture was on the cover of a couple of magazines that year.

When Bob thought about it, he realized that was actually a typical year. It was one of the years when he was reaching for every brass ring on the merry-go-round. Somewhere along the line, he stopped reaching. Of course, by then his daughter was already in college.

Sometimes people ask him if he was able to regain the time, to rebuild the lost relationship with his daughter. "The answer is no," he says. "It's like asking how well you made a first impression the second time. You only get one chance. If you blow it, it's gone."

Bob still has copies of the magazines with his picture on them. Someday, he will show them to his daughter. But he wishes he had a picture of himself in a baseball cap with his hand on the shoulder of a little girl missing her baby teeth instead.

Most of us, most of the time, enjoy our work. It gives us challenge and structure. Our work strengthens our identity and gives us a reason to get up in the morning. We work hard for our families. It's true that our family shares in our success. But if we are not careful, they also pay the price.

How do we balance our professional and personal lives, providing for our families without losing them in the process? We admire Olympians for their singular focus and their intense concentration on a goal. Olympians give up their whole lives for the chance to stand on the medal podium, gold heavy around their necks, hands on hearts as their national anthems play. Our judo Olympians carry the weight of the sport on their shoulders. They are largely self-funded, relying on donations, selling tee shirts and posters to raise money. These athletes scrimp and scrape, sacrificing critical career-building years to make the Olympic team. Often they put off finishing college and delay marrying and starting families.

Unlike many athletes who put their lives on hold when pursuing the Olympic dream, Jimmy Pedro, three-time Olympian and 1999 World Champion, adopted a different philosophy. "Although judo was the most important part of my life, I decided that I would not make it my whole life," he explains. "I found the person I wanted to spend my whole life with—why delay? I've shared my life, good and bad, with my wife and kids. Winning and losing are empty without someone to share it with."

Providing for our families without losing them in the process

"Balance is the biggest challenge for someone in a major leadership role. It is a struggle to spend time with the family for evening meals and vacations."
Wendell Strode

In the corporate world, balance challenges are compounded with today's leaner staffs and longer hours. Work can become a never-ending, never-satisfied addiction, demanding all our time and energy. Technology and the virtual office can make it nearly impossible to turn off. Laptops, the internet and cell phones allow you to work anywhere, any hour of the day so we find ourselves working everywhere, all hours of the day. We even work on vacation, calling into the office for critical messages, checking email from Internet cafes in Europe. Technology has tethered us to the office. "Work can be like a drug – it takes discipline to shut it off. With cell phones, emails, and faxes I could work 24 hours per day," says Jim Carrick.

In the quiet hours after everyone else has left the office, the temptation is strong to stay a little longer. We call home and say, "I'll leave the office in 15 minutes," then stay just a bit longer, just long enough to make a few more phone calls, to clear out email or empty an inbox. Before we know it, staying late becomes commonplace. Missed dinners with our family are replaced by wolfing down leftovers at the kitchen counter. We collapse into our favorite easy chair, drained from the day's work, too tired for conversation, wanting no more than to vegetate in front of the television.

We race through our weekends, packed full of home projects, grocery shopping and carpooling the kids. We wear our busyness like a badge of honor. With all this busyness we allow friendships to drift away, unable to commit the time and emotional energy to sustain them. This busyness doesn't necessarily create a fuller life. Our non-stop activity and over-commitment fray the bonds holding together our marriages and families.

Putting balance on a back burner

On those rare moments of reflection, we question the value of our over-committed schedule, "Has this become my life? Work, eat, sleep, is this really all there is?" Reflection often brings unpleasant realities and the nagging thought that we have been racing toward the wrong goal.

Yet, it is difficult to keep any perspective when so much of our life and social network is wrapped up in work. Frequent relocations isolate us from community and extended family support. When all of our friends are from the office, the company becomes our second family.

Confronting the problems of our personal lives is unpleasant. It is far easier to work compulsively. We can become addicted to work when it is such a large part of our identity and such a powerful source of positive strokes.

For some, it takes a lay-off to provide a quiet time to think things through, to take a fresh look at life away from the influence of corporate thinking. Down time can also come through a leave of absence or a break between jobs, giving us a chance to catch our breath and gain a new perspective.

Because pausing to re-evaluate our priorities and direction in life can be discomforting we prefer to put the future on a back burner. We think, "I will live in balance when things slow down a little at work, when my staff is not so lean, when I complete this big project or reach the next level." We weigh the short-term sacrifice, sure that we can live in balance later.

We climb the ladder to a level of success, catch our breath and look around. "Okay, life," we say, "I'm ready to balance." Only to find that years of too much travel, too many exhausting workweeks, and too many years without a vacation have taken their toll. "It's sad that as I turned 50 I achieved greater balance in my life but now the kids are gone. They turned out just like me in the maniacal pursuit of work," says Jim McCallie.

Barriers to balance

"I used to say, take care of the company and it will take care of you. Now I say, take care of yourself and the company will do just fine."
Catherine Weeks

What is keeping you from a balanced life? It's easy to blame the company. It's true that some big name organizations deliberately burn through people because they know there is always a fresh supply of talent eager to sign on with their successful image.

That supply is even greater in the aftermath of massive lay-offs. The unemployment rate for managers and professionals is at a level not seen since the white-collar lay-offs of the early 1990s. And the days of full employment and competing job offers in the late 1990s now seem like light years ago as companies continue to cut back in the face of flat demand. Companies everywhere are doing more work with fewer people, leaving many fearful of losing their jobs or being demoted if they are perceived as lacking total commitment?

It's difficult to step off the fast track and walk away from joining the inner circle. As I became more involved in athletics and coaching, climbing the corporate ladder lost much of its appeal. I was happy to work hard and make a contribution, but I was no longer willing to make further sacrifices to get farther.

Yet the decision to plateau my career was difficult. I had always been driven by ambition and the need to prove myself. Athletics allowed me to channel those energies and ambitions in a different direction.

Have you reached a point where you can be content to stay at your current level? What would you be willing to give up to live in balance? Could you cut back on a long commute, take another position that didn't require so much travel, work for a smaller company in a community with a slower pace of life? What would you be willing to trade for a better quality of life for you and your family? Can you simplify your lifestyle and reduce your commitments? The answers to some of these questions may be no. You may not be ready for balance.

Look at it from another perspective. What would you do to earn more money? Would you relocate away from extended family to a bigger city? Would you work most weekends and travel every week? Would you give up vacations? Would you give up on your marriage or even your kids? Often we don't think through what we are putting at risk when we accept promotions or relocations. We don't weigh the true cost of our success. We don't realize that each career choice we make takes us away from one path and toward another life.

Each choice takes us closer or farther

"The biggest decision of my life was to move from Florida to New Jersey to become president of the North East division. It was a great opportunity for the company and for my career. I believe there are no right or wrong decisions, only the decisions we make. Ultimately it cost me my marriage. It was a very bad time for the kids and for me. I tried to go home on weekends, but your family doesn't wait for you; they have their own lives."
Larry Mercer

Are your choices taking you toward a fulfilling future? The painful realities of the recession have added to our financial stress. We used to say money was the most easily renewable resource, but the stock market has lost $9 trillion in value since the fall of 2000. Job anxiety has soared among white-collar workers. Small pay raises are offset by worker's share of rapidly rising health costs, shrinking performance bonuses and underwater stock options. Personal bankruptcies are at an all time high.

Even without a recession, debt shackles many to an unbalanced life? Our society is crazed with consumerism, with acquiring the latest gadgets, the biggest houses on the block and highest status vehicles. We try to consume ourselves to contentment and then expend more time and energy taking care of all of our possessions. No matter what we earn, we manage to spend even more. How much money is enough? If we keep our heads down and work away to pay the bills, we will always live just beyond our means. We will never catch up, never catch our breath, and never change our lives. Consumerism is out of control when it keeps us from living our lives with purpose.

When I was a student at The Ohio State University, the sure sign of success was to own a house in a golf course community called Muirfield. On Sunday afternoons, we would drive through the subdivision and dream about making it big and owning one of the large, expensive houses. Later, I learned many of the homes were empty. Fresh out of college, newly married two-career couples would go deep into debt to buy a house. With no money left for furniture, they slept on a mattress in one of the bedrooms. More than a shell of a house, it was a shell of a life.

Dave Ramsey has devoted his life to helping people free themselves from debt and find financial peace. Thousands have participated in his twelve-week program, Financial Peace University.

In his nationally syndicated radio show, The Money Game, Dave advises callers to take "seven financial baby steps:"

1. Save $1,000 in an emergency fund.
2. Pay off all debt except the mortgage.
3. Complete your emergency fund by saving three to six months expenses.
4. Fully fund your pretax retirement savings.
5. Save for your kids' college.
6. Pay off your home early.
7. Build wealth and give like crazy.

The trigger to re-evaluate

"I am a recovering workaholic. In the early part of my career, I emphasized work above all else. Not taking vacations is not a value to pride yourself on. I found a different perspective after my husband was diagnosed with kidney cancer. Illness brings up mortality issues and what is really important. But as time slipped away from the surgery it was easy to resume prior practices. The trigger makes you realize what is truly important, but it fades with time."
Nancy Haslip

People often reach a new realization after suffering a life crisis: divorce, a serious illness or downsizing. After a traumatic event, people often take time for reflection and to re-prioritize their lives. Sometimes the trigger to seek balance comes in time to ward off impending crises—an affair, alcoholism, burnout or depression.

As a country we experienced a collective crisis on 09/11. A Time/CNN poll two months after the 09/11 attack found that 62% wanted to spend more time with family; and 55% felt a greater purpose in life.[4] But for many, 09/11 led to good intentions and promises not kept.

As the shock wore off and the headlines changed, life returned to normal. How many of us made new choices? Despite our very best intentions, did we change our lives? As we celebrate weddings and graduations in the bright spring days that seem a lifetime removed from 9/11, how often do we pause to take measure of what is most important?

My trigger to re-evaluate my life choices was not one large dramatic event, but rather a series of small events that led to an unmistakable conclusion.

I began seriously considering balance as my marriage unraveled in the mid-1990s, at the same time Stephen Covey's book, *The Seven Habits of Highly Effective People*, was climbing the bestseller charts. I agreed with him in principle, but couldn't see how I could fit balance into my already overcrowded life. I attended a Covey seminar with several of my managers. After lunch, Covey spoke on putting first things first. I heard him, really heard him, for the first time.

As the meaning of his words sank in, I remembered that my daughter had stayed home sick from school that morning, all alone in our trophy house. There didn't seem to be a better time to find balance. I left the seminar and drove home to my daughter, still in her pajamas.

I knew it was likely that I had lost my marriage but I was determined not to lose my daughter. She was already 13, with only a few years of parenting remaining. I had already missed out on so much of her childhood, I wanted to be there to guide her through the teenage years.

At Home Depot, we had what we called "Depot divorces." It wasn't that the company demanded your entire life. The problem was that the company we were building was so exciting it was all consuming. It was hard for spouses to understand the long hours, the constant travel, the bonding of the team. We traveled together, ate and slept at a thousand different hotels. Work became a blur of cities with the stores the only constant.

As my marriage unraveled, I closed my eyes to the obvious signs. Consumed with anxiety, I retreated to work, logging longer hours, traveling more to fill up the void, keeping frantically busy so there was no time to think. I couldn't slow down because that meant coming to terms with the truth. My daughter struggled through adolescence alone.

One night, flying home over Dallas, famous for its thunderstorms, our plane flew into the mouth of a monster. The plane bucked and rolled violently as the pilots fought to keep control. No one said a word as we gripped our armrests tightly and prayed. The flight attendants' faces blanched white with fear as they sat crouched into little balls on their jump seats. With lightening flashing outside my window, I bargained with God. "Lord, Lord, if you get me on the ground safely, I will change my life." I meant it.

The following bright, blue-sky morning I sat in my living room. A dogwood bloomed a snowfall of white blossoms outside the bay window. Sunlight flooded the room in bright rectangular patches, burnishing the antiques, glinting off the ebony grand piano in the corner. The richness of the room stood in stark contrast to the emptiness of my marriage.

I kept my promise, though my heart ached. The words stuck in my throat. I asked, "Do you want a divorce?"

We sought marriage counseling at our church. But it was obvious to everyone, except our young, unmarried counselor that the marriage was badly broken. I told myself, "If I can just be home every night for dinner, we can rebuild our marriage." I did not want the failure of divorce.

Consumed with anxiety over my disintegrating marriage, I could not concentrate on my work, could not consistently lead my managers, the best and brightest in the country. I failed. It broke my heart to leave Depot. I went into my boss's office twice to resign but could not finish for the grief at the thought of leaving. I was determined to never again fall in love with a company; to never again cry over anything that couldn't cry over me.

I stepped off the fast track and out of the spotlight and hid out in rural Kentucky, accepting an offer with Dollar General. It was in Kentucky that my marriage finally failed. My small town lawyer had a kind heart. He was obligated to ask me, "Is the marriage irrevocably broken?" And I was obligated to answer, "Yes."

I spent that first Christmas alone in Kentucky, far from family and friends. I tried to comfort myself as I fed the dogs and waited out the endless holiday. "I tried my best to save my marriage," I told the dogs and they wagged their tails in agreement. It was true. But it was cold comfort.

Sometimes, we give up marriages and, even worse, our children, for the love of a company. We get so caught up in the game, in our own career, in the next success. We think, if I can make it to the next level, the intensity will wear off, things will slow down. Then I can spend more time with family. We don't stop to ask, what will I lose with all of this winning?

Regaining our balance

"Family comes first. I work hard at leaving the office on time. During the workday, I focus 100% on my work. At home I focus 100% on my family. I may work some more on my laptop after the kids are asleep, but I spend time with the children. I won't know if it is enough until they grow up."
Bertie Wherley

A career is not enough to build your life around. Every career will have its mountains and valleys. When you are deep in one of the valleys, you'll appreciate a multi-dimensional life. You can shift from a single focus to a full life. You can become involved in your community, develop a rewarding family life, and leave a lasting contribution.

By living your life in balance, you not only positively affect your family and community but all the people who will work for you over a 40-year career. It is critical to recognize that balance is more than multi-tasking, more than cleverly cramming more into each day. Most of us are already overworked and overwhelmed by multiple roles and responsibilities. Balance is more than compartmentalizing our roles as professionals, parents and spouses.

For each of us, balance is a personal matter, driven by our values and goals. Our definition of balance changes over time with different stages of our lives. When our children are small, it is most important to give them a solid grounding. Empty nesters, on the other hand, can commit fully to their profession. We wobble out of balance when we live our lives in opposition to our goals and values.

Balance begins by taking an inventory of your life. As we reach mid-life, we learn that we have a finite supply of time and energy. It takes pacing and prioritization to last through the long haul. Balance comes from asking the hard questions and honestly evaluating the answers, from forgiving your mistakes and making peace with your past. You can't undo what has been damaged, but you can start fresh, and do better tomorrow.

Balance begins by being clear on your end purpose. Quickly write down your top three personal and professional goals:

Top three personal goals:

    1.

    2.

    3.

Top three professional goals:

    1.

    2.

    3.

Ask yourself: "What do I want to achieve in life? Is ambition still burning brightly, driving me toward career success? Or have I reached a level of success that allows me to relax and enjoy what I've accomplished?"

What is the most important thing to you? Will the things you're working on today still be important next week, next month, next year?

Are you pursing your goals or someone else's? Do your professional goals fit your personal sense of purpose?

Are you in harmony with your spouse and your life goals or are you drifting through life without goals, merely reacting to opportunity and crises?

Are your top three personal and professional goals in conflict? Look at the example below – what is wrong with this example?

Top three personal goals:

1. A strong, happy marriage.
2. Three happy, healthy children.
3. Personal growth and development.

Top three professional goals:

1. Director of Fortune 500 by age 35.
2. Annual base salary of $100,000 by age 35.
3. National professional reputation.

Some would argue that there is no conflict between these personal and professional goals. Others would say these goals are achievable with a stay at home spouse. Check your goals for hidden conflicts keeping you from balance

Next, check your goals against the price you are willing to pay.

The price I am willing to pay:

1.

2.

3.

Price unwilling to pay:

1.

2.

3.

Is the payoff from your top three personal and professional goals worth the price?

Using our previous top three professional goals example, this person might list the following:

The price I am willing to pay:

1. Work 12 and 16 hour days, five days per week, occasionally six days per week.
2. Travel 2 to 3 days per week.
3. Relocate every 18 to 24 months.

Price unwilling to pay:

1. Work 7 days per week.
2. Travel 75% of the time.
3. Put undue stress and strain on marriage.

Next, list the time and money spent last week next to each one of your personal and professional goals. Are you putting energy and resources toward your end result?

Top three personal goals:	**Time spent**	**Money spent**
1.		
2.		
3.		
Top three professional goals:	**Time spent**	**Money spent**
1.		
2.		
3.		

In chapter two, you listed your top ten personal and professional values. Whittle those down to the final four in each category and match them against your goals. Do your values match up to your goals?

Take a hard look at the person you are becoming. If you stay on this path, what will your life look like five, ten or twenty years down the road?

Often it is difficult to see how the actions we take today affect our future. For example, when I first started judo, I was an unskilled and overweight white belt. My only athletic goal as a white belt was to lose weight and earn my yellow belt. By practicing three times per week, competing, coaching and refereeing, I became a black belt in five years. I didn't realize how my sport would shape my philosophy and change my life. This exercise can help you determine how your life will change. If you continue to do X, in five years you will have become Y. Do you like the person you are becoming?

Taking baby steps toward balance

"I didn't know about balance early in my career. I was a workaholic. I drove myself to the point that I dropped with a heart attack. Then I took the time to reassess what is important in life - spending time with family, church and community. It takes an emotional toll if you cannot be there for family. As a leader, you must demonstrate these values. Spending time in the evening with a briefcase full of work is foolish. You cannot go into work the next morning refreshed. If you work twelve-hour days and every weekend, ask yourself, is this what I want out of life? I learned these lessons the hard way after a heart attack."
Bernie Hale

I led a roundtable discussion with a group of downsized executives on September 10, 2001. The date was not important except in retrospect, one day before the country re-examined its priorities. With one exception, this group of motivated, ambitious, well-educated executives had decided to accept their next assignment to achieve greater balance. Their reasons varied: some had young children, others cared for aging parents, a few had faced a health scare. After being laid off and going through a period of re-adjustment to a lower budget lifestyle, they found they wanted more time than money. Unwilling to work 80-hour weeks or travel constantly, they were consciously choosing to scale back at work, to simplify their lives and live at a less frantic pace.

Several spoke of different priorities earlier in their careers, of having a different definition of success. Now they were focused toward family. They still wanted success, but on their own terms. These outsourced executives, all highly marketable, all successful, were taking control of their careers and their lives.

Have you figured out the difference between what you want versus what you need? The next time you say you are working so hard and sacrificing for your children, ask yourself if you would want your child to work for your company and live your life.

Thinking through what you want out of life versus how you are living today is the first step in making necessary changes before you experience a crisis. Realizing you've allowed relationships to fail because all your energy has gone to busyness and accumulating wealth and success will help you pace yourself. Putting time and energy toward your goals guarantees that the important gets done. The rest simply stays undone. Instead of admiring busyness, view your friends and colleagues' overscheduled, frantic lives with a shudder of sympathy. Choose not to cram every moment full with activity. Drive slowly on occasion. Allow people to get in line in front of you. Say, "I'm not in a hurry," until you believe it.

We know from our earliest management training that we manage what we can measure. Instead of wishing you could be home in time for dinner more often or travel less frequently, write down specific goals. Start with baby steps—mini-goals you can achieve, even under stress.

Write specific goals in your daily planner each week—to be home three nights a week, to travel no more than one week per month. Schedule regular time to exercise or commit hours to volunteer work that feeds your spirit.

If you carry work home every night, set a goal to only take home your stuffed briefcase every other night. If you work every weekend, begin giving yourself one day off each weekend to rest and recharge your batteries. Dedicate a portion of each weekend to family time, and set aside time just for yourself to relax. Having goals and time targets that you can measure will keep you focused on your commitments and give you a feeling of control over your life.

Schedule your friends and family time into your daily planner with the same dedication you plan for an important meeting. When tempting opportunities come along, check them against your values and goals. You'll quickly determine if the opportunity takes you away from or moves you toward your priorities.

For all of us, September 11th was a wakeup call. If life can be cut short, it is important to live it well. If careers can be uncertain, it is critical to have a full life with family and friends. Don't wait for balance until the mortgage is paid off and the kids are out of college. Live now, in this moment. Make the changes you need to live a full life.

This is your life—live it by your terms. Let the priorities in your life fill the hours in your day and your daily planner. Develop a life that measures success by your standards. Keep a strong sense of who you are and what your life is all about. Let go of things that keep you from living on purpose. We can't turn the clock back and we can never get that time back. But we can learn from each life lesson. We can learn from Kathleen.

Kathleen's story

"I am a six year cancer survivor. Having an illness gives me the freedom to re-examine my priorities. All of those years I worked instead of taking care of myself caught up with me. I felt the effect of the stress from working too many hours and protecting the people who worked for me. Those years took a toll. I took a step back to reduce stress. Now I have a whole new outlook on life – a new balance between work and personal."
Kathleen Strange

Kathleen Strange was a pioneer in the logistics field. She carved out a career in the late 1970s in the rapidly changing, male dominated field of logistics, becoming a vice president for several Fortune 500 companies. Kathleen was my role model for a dozen years as I followed in her career footsteps.

In our first interview for this book, Kathleen mentioned almost casually that she was a cancer survivor. Subsequent interviews took on a different tone; we spent less time on pleasantries, devoted more effort to capturing what Kathleen had learned. She didn't regret the choices or the sacrifices she had made for her career, but said simply, "Too much of my life has been devoted to work. I sit in my office at 8 p.m. and think, I could not have a family."

"I gave my all to the organization—I thought there would be a payoff at the end, that the organization would reward me. But there was only a lesson," she said. Kathleen left the organization and 110-hour, seven-day work weeks behind. She chose a boss she admired, chose a company that valued both hard work and having a personal life.

But it was too late. Her body was weakened from overwork, lack of exercise, and too many late nights of grabbing sandwiches out of vending machines. After her diagnosis, Kathleen focused on strengthening her body to survive the cancer. She began asking, what do I want to be remembered for? "I have done a lot of looking inward to learn and to grow. It is the work of a life time," Kathleen said. "It is how you live your life that matters." Fully a career woman, she admired and supported her sister's and sister-in-law's decisions to stay at home with their children.

I saw Kathleen briefly at a conference last fall. She was back in treatment, wearing a headscarf. We waved across a crowded room but didn't get a chance to talk. I met one of her colleagues this spring, and sent back a note of encouragement. But it was too late. Kathleen Strange passed on April 19, 2002.

When I got the call, I paused in my work. It seemed wrong to stay at my desk. But maybe it was right to focus on her message. For a long while, I stared out the window at the newly planted fields, the gnarled old trees that once stood sentry to fields as far as the eye could see, now crowded with houses. I paused – breathed a prayer for Kathleen, and wrote.

Chapter Three

Leadership Questions

- What does it mean to live in balance?

- How do you define success?

- What sacrifices have you made for your career? Was it worth it?

- Would you like your children to follow in your professional footsteps?

- How do you balance your commitments between work, family and community?

- What advice would you give to young people just starting their careers?

Chapter Four

The Courage of Character

Fall 1997

In the fall of 1997, on a cold, starless night, my life changed in a split second. My judo partner threw hard, and in that split-second of reaction time, something went wrong. I landed hard. Everything went black. And then I went numb.

As the assistant coach knelt over me, I couldn't feel my arms and legs. In the eternity it took for the ambulance to arrive, I lay there motionless on the mat, staring up at the lights. Tears trickled down my face. I thought, "What have I done? Will I ever walk again?" My judo partner knelt beside me, "Be brave, Rebecca, be brave," she kept repeating.

The emergency technicians strapped me into a neck brace and lifted me onto a stretcher. The ambulance raced to the emergency room, sirens blaring. After countless X-rays were taken, I lay strapped onto a cold metal table, alone, awaiting the results.

When sensei walked into the room, his eyes shone bright blue with relief. He took my hand and helped me sit up. That small movement held such freedom. The doctors told us the shock of the fall had traumatized my spine, causing temporary paralysis and tearing my back muscles. It would take 18 months to heal.

During those long, lonely winter nights of recovery, I had a lot of time to think. I looked deep inside. Why was winning that gold medal so important to me? Was it worth the risks? Was it for the right reasons?

I knew that, in the big scheme of things, winning a gold medal would not change my life. It would not make me rich and famous. I would not smile at the world from the cover of the Wheaties box.

But I realized it meant more than a gold medal to me. As we reach mid life, we start thinking about our legacy. What will we leave behind? I knew there had to be more meaning to life than advancing my own career, more than building material wealth.

More than a gold medal, I was searching for my purpose; for what would make my life matter. Could I make a difference in other people's lives?

It wasn't just the gold medal. It was about living with character and courage.

Sensei reminded me, "In judo, as in life, there is a difference between pain and injury. You must never surrender. Because if you can withstand the pain and keep fighting, you may go on to win the gold."

I started rehabilitation immediately, making twice weekly rounds to the physical therapist and chiropractor. I returned to judo a week after the accident to watch practice. A few weeks later, I was back at practice, my arm tied to my side with my orange belt to immobilize the right side of my body. Some nights I lasted only 15 minutes before my back gave out. I would retreat to the edge of the mat in tears of pain and frustration, sitting out the rest of practice. I spent non-practice nights on the couch with a heating pad, willing my back to heal quickly.

For a year and a half, I healed. Through the pain and sweat and recovery, I matured as an athlete and as a leader. When I returned to full practice after the injury, I was a different person. I had a new certainty and calmness of purpose. I was doing judo for my love of the sport, not for a gold medal, not for sensei's approval. I was doing it for me.

But it wasn't easy. I had to start all over and learn to do techniques left-handed. I had to push past discouragement and the darkness of self-doubt. I had to overcome the bitterness of being hurt.

After the injury, every time I competed I was gripped with fear. I would stand at the edge of the mat, trembling with fear and adrenalin. I learned that sometimes you have to dig down deep to find your courage. In the years that followed, I trained hard, got hurt and kept training. I competed and won matches and lost matches and kept fighting because, for an athlete, the very worst thing is to know you gave it your all and your all was not enough. Facing down that fear takes courage. The courage it took to give my all and return to the mat is the same courage that took me away from a corporate career.

The case for courage

"There is no pivotal moment, only small acts of courage for the right decision."
Jim Carrick

We often think of courage in terms of one-time heroic acts of war or in the bravery of the firefighters who risked - and too often gave - their lives on September 11th.

But courage in the large acts comes from courage built from a series of small acts. James Bregman, 1964 Olympian, says, "The real courage is what you do on a daily basis, how you conduct yourself to the standards you have set. That will lead to doing the right thing and the next right thing. The more times you do the next right thing, the more ingrained proper conduct becomes. It starts with little things and ends with big things."

Over 100 interviews with business leaders showed clearly that this type of courage is essential for long-term career success and personal satisfaction. Without courage, you live a less full life. You don't go as far in your career or last as long. But just as some people aren't sure if they have an identity apart from their job title, some aren't sure they have values apart from what the company has given them. Others simply aren't strong enough. It takes courage to follow your values and be unwavering. But a career without courage flattens out because it is not built on a solid foundation.

It is critical that courage become a core value of the company because the organization pays the price for the misconduct of a few: lawsuits, front-page scandals and punishment of the price per share. Putting aside Enron, which seems corrupt throughout its culture, most companies would welcome the opportunity to correct problems before they hit the headlines giving the organization a public black eye and besmirched reputation. It is in the company's best interests to develop courage in its leaders because only the largest organizations can afford to staff ethics officer positions and ethics hotlines. The rest must rely on their employees to do what is right and report what is wrong.

Organizational integrity begins with the organization's framework of values and ends with individual accountability. Nine in ten employees say they expect their organizations to do what is right, not just what is profitable. The same percentage say the people they work with believe in the organization's standards and values.[1] As their leaders, we must live and breathe our values, modeling them in everyday behavior.

Courage is needed in transition

"In my former company, they put values into operations across the entire organization. But when the merger was announced, the importance of values stopped and today values are not espoused."
Anonymous

As mentioned in chapter one, when times are the toughest, integrity matters the most. The 2000 Ethics Resource Center study showed that companies in transition from mergers and acquisitions, restructuring or lay-offs are associated with higher levels of misconduct. [2] The percentage of employees who observed misconduct in the past year was 37% for transitioning organizations compared to 27% of employees who worked in stable organizations.[3] Why the higher rates of misconduct?

Change, stress and high stakes bring out the best and worst in human behavior. Organizational transitions redefine organizational priorities and disrupt reporting relationships and patterns of communication, resulting in uncertainty and stress.[4] The loss of a trusted supervisor, increased workload and additional responsibilities can cause employees to question company norms. During tough economic times, especially during lay-offs when employee cynicism reaches an all time high, companies can be challenged to live by their values.

Sometimes it seems like we are working in different organizations. Senior and middle managers observe less misconduct, feel less pressure to compromise integrity and are more likely to report misconduct.[5] High level employees and senior mangers also have more positive perceptions of the ethical behavior of their leaders than do lower level employees.[6] We tend to overestimate our employee's commitment to company values and underestimate the company's risk. We grow overconfident that the scandals we read about and watch on TV couldn't happen here.

Courage is needed to question

"There is a lot of fear for advancement, for the job. This causes people to look the other way. If someone is driven by money and financial gain, they will be more desperate when faced with losing a job."
Barbara Best

There are many reasons why it could happen here, but only two main reasons why your employees wouldn't report misconduct or raise concerns. 34% are afraid they will be seen as a troublemaker by management.[7] 35% fear their coworkers will see them as a "snitch." In transitioning organizations experiencing lay-offs, the percentage climbs to 42%.[8] Even among senior and middle managers, one in five say they will be seen as troublemakers by management if they report misconduct.[9] These discouraging percentages speak to a deep distrust of management.

These fears appear to be justified. Unlike Enron whistle blower, Sherron Watkins, who was widely praised for her highly developed moral sense and incredible courage, [10] most "snitches" are quietly fired, their careers derailed, their reputations ruined.

Nina Aversano, former president of sales for North America, claimed she was fired in retaliation for giving detailed warning that Lucent's sales targets were unrealistic. Lucent improperly booked $679 million in revenue during its 2000 fiscal year, boosting sales revenues by giving credit to customers unlikely to pay and counting sales for product shipped to distribution partners that was never sold to end customers. Lucent stock lost 77% of its value in the one year period between their first earnings warning and the formal SEC investigation.[11]

Former Xerox finance executive, James F. Bingham, sued the company for wrongful termination, claiming he was fired in August 2000 because he tried to call attention to accounting fraud. His complaint alleged that Chief Financial Officer, Barry Romeril directed underlings to boost income by selling banks the rights to future revenues from Xerox copiers that were on short-term rentals to customers. When KPMG declined to certify Xerox's financial results, the company delayed filing its annual report, which prompted a widening probe by the SEC.[12] Almost two years later, Xerox admitted to inflating revenue by $1.9 billion.

Clearly it is in the company's best interest to have early warning and an opportunity to make the situation right. Most people are doing their best to lead honorably on a day-by-day basis; most companies stumble and fall due to radioactive influence of a few. Unfortunately, many companies don't find out about misconduct in time to correct it because of the stigma of whistle blowing. A study conducted by Walker Information revealed that nearly a third of employees believe whistle blowing on illegal or unethical company actions is, in itself, a serious ethical violation.[13]

We have grown accustomed to accounting scandals: Rite Aid, Sunbeam and Waste Management were precursors to Enron. Normally, accounting fraud takes months, if not years, to unravel; the charges are complicated and the heroes and villains are painted in shades of gray rather than black and white. SEC investigations are cumbersome, requiring lengthy probes into complex financial arrangements. The scandal plays out in the press amid a flurry of lawsuits by former employees and shareholders and counter accusations of incompetent leadership.

Unlike these highly visible cases, most misconduct is garden variety, according to a 2000 study by the Ethics Resource Center.[14]

Types of misconduct:

Lying to employees, customers, vendors or the public.	26%
Withholding needed information from employees, customers, vendors or the public.	25%
Abusive or intimidating behavior towards employees.	24%
Misreporting actual time or hours worked.	21%
Discrimination on the basis of race, color, gender, age or similar categories.	17%

Even small companies with high integrity leadership are not immune. Mike almost lost his advertising agency to employee fear. An employee was stealing money from the company by cutting phony invoices and pocketing the money. Other employees saw the dishonesty and knew the company was being cheated, but thought the owners might be in on it. They were afraid they might lose their job if they mentioned it.   So they did nothing. Eventually one person came forward.

Mike prosecuted the thief, whose excuse was that he felt he was worth more than he was being paid. Mike said, "I think I was more disappointed to find out that other employees knew about it but did nothing. I wear my values on my sleeve. They should have known by my character."

The faces of courage

We are not accustomed to talking about courage in leadership except in the abstract, occasionally anchored to examples: he has the courage of his convictions, she has the courage to keep the course despite crushing pressure, he has the courage to make the tough decisions without consultants.

There are many types of quiet courage, many unreported examples and small moments. Courage is doing what is right for the organization and its people when there are no easy answers. Courage is called on when there is pressure to compromise, to look the other way or to give in to the urgency of an unfilled position with a questionable candidate.

Sometimes courage comes when your back is against the wall and you cannot retreat one more step, when you have to dig down deep to find your courage.

But courage is not charging ahead on a Quixotic mission at all costs. That is closer to being a loose cannon, both reckless and foolish. Sometimes we romanticize the notion of going down in flames fighting for right, but the reality is that your people benefit far more from your continued leadership. Courage is closer to taking measured risks, arguing your case intelligently and occasionally coming back to fight another day.

The courage to challenge

"I was put in the penalty box – they didn't kill me, but put me where I couldn't hurt the agenda."
Jim McCallie

Courage is doing what is right for the organization when it is risky or unpopular. It takes courage to challenge the status quo, to change the business model and push change through resistance. But courage grows when you are tested; when you make a decision that puts your reputation and career at stake.

"Going through the fire and being pushed to the edge teaches you how to respond to conflict in real business issues. You have to believe in yourself," says Tim (a pseudonym).

Tim was 25 when he put a halt on a new system rollout, putting his career on the line to stabilize the system and pushing a million dollar bleed up through the organization. Without years of experience to anchor him, he worked off sheer intuition and his internal compass to decide what was right for the organization.

Tim was the only product person on the team – the others in information technology were under heavy incentives to get the system online quickly.

The business was highly seasonal and the team was under pressure to have the system up and running by the holidays. The team tested the pilot system at one site and found problems. At first, they weren't sure if the problems were with the system or the users. But after testing the system at a second site, they discovered a number of major design flaws in the guts of the application.

Tim had to articulate the unpopular. He was going to shut the system down for six months until it could be stabilized - a million dollar delay. The IT group accused him of "scope creep" - of changing the requirements - and recommended to senior management that his group do a better job of keeping track of inventory.

They spent six months stabilizing the pilot system and then began to roll it out. This time it worked. "After that, even though I still have lots of stress - even though there are things that burn a hole in my gut - being tested made me more sure of myself," he says.

The courage to confront

"What do leaders need most? Strong followers."
Troy Fellers

We often think of courage in terms of leadership, but courage is also needed for followship because many people become fearful during change. Those lacking courage won't speak up when their company is headed in the wrong direction. Confused between courage and loyalty, they won't confront their boss. That is a failure of followship far more serious than any disloyalty. It is not a disservice to challenge if you've given your boss loyalty in the little things, years of trustworthy service and a strong track record. It is not disloyal to question a course of action that puts the company at risk. Rather, it is timid and irresponsible to not challenge the consequences of bad decisions.

Getting on the wrong side of management - going against the momentum toward a misguided goal - can be extremely uncomfortable. But companies and their leadership make mistakes. Even the very best ones are a work in progress. It is up to you to challenge and change the company for the better.

To become strong leaders, we have to be willing to challenge and to be challenged. It takes courage to solicit feedback and act on criticism. But one in three employees who feel pressure attributes it to their supervisor or top management. Leaders with the most power are perceived to exert the greatest pressure on others to compromise their integrity. As leaders, we reflect the organization. We must provide the opportunity for our followers to speak up.

There are many who think it is safest to never speak up, safest not to rock the boat. They are the same people who never make waves or go out on a limb; the "yes men" who are widely disrespected within the organization. Those lacking courage will wind up getting by without getting results. People can be well networked and successful by material standards. But without courage, cynicism creeps through.

An acquaintance illustrates this chameleon-like behavior. Whatever his boss said, he was in complete agreement. Whatever the flavor of the day, that was his favorite. He was not a bad person - for the most part he was harmless, even amusing, until the day his boss was put in a position of great authority.

This boss was a weak leader who depended on his followers. Based on their enthusiastic support, he made a disastrous decision that led to a series of events that, in turn, caused the company to lose millions, miss its earnings targets and see its share prices tumble. When it was all over, several careers had been ruined and dozens in management had lost their stock option retirement cushions.

This man still works for the company. He was not wholly responsible – he is just a man whose lack of courage to confront issues cost his co-workers, his company and its shareholders. Yet every night he gets into his luxury car and drives to his executive house, home to his wife and young son. I've often wondered, how does he look into the eyes of his son? What kind of man will he raise him to be?

The courage of character

"If one is purely materialist, how satisfying can that be? How can you respect yourself? They will eventually have health problems from the stress of fighting themselves."
Barbara Best

It takes courage to do what is right for the organization when there are high stakes of money, power and stock options at risk. My accountant tells me that if you want to know the character of a person, talk to her about her money. She will sit in her office and tell you things she's done and justify it by saying, "That's business."

A friend of mine, an investment broker, uses the same phrase. Last week he sat at my kitchen table. He looked exhausted, but he shrugged and said, "That's business." He had sold a high-risk investment to a client in Canada - who subsequently lost $60,000.

My friend couldn't fall asleep until 2 a.m. that morning thinking about his client in Canada and the lost $60,000 that would have been his daughter's college tuition.

My friend is a man of character. He supports a pregnant wife and has no health insurance. He badly needs his job. But the call from Canada was the second call that week. And he can't sleep at night. So he is resigning his position.

My investment broker, on the other hand, has never lost a moment's sleep over all the money I've lost. And I tell you that you cannot separate work from home and say "That's business." You must lead with courage and character in all parts of your life.

The courage to lead

"My boss folded like an accordion in front of the big boss."
Doug Fortune

While courage in followship is important, courage is also needed for leadership. When employees perceive their leaders setting a good example of integrity, they feel less pressure to compromise integrity, observe less misconduct, are more satisfied with their organization and feel more valued.15 How big a difference does this make? 93% of employees who agree that the head of their organization "sets a good example of ethical business behavior" say they are satisfied with their organizations.16

Courage is critical to leadership because people will not respect or follow a leader who will not stand up for them. It takes courage to fight for your people, to represent them when they can't speak for themselves. Both at home and at work, people are motivated by feelings of belonging and loyalty.

Jane (a pseudonym) was 28 when she faced the most difficult situation in her life. She found out that the owner of a distribution center had been stealing millions of dollars in materials from her company. As Jane investigated and dug deeper, she discovered that he had been kiting checks between several businesses he owned. Facing jail time on charges of theft and fraud, the owner committed suicide.

The man's workers blamed Jane and her company. Jane and her team flew to the site to manage the distribution center until they could close it down. The employees were disgruntled and dangerous - the second shift employees were prisoners on work release.

Jane called corporate and requested security. Her boss told her not to pull her team out, not to leave until they could shut down the operation. But the security they sent was one elderly rent-a-cop.

Jane was torn between her obligation to the organization and her promise to protect her people. She struggled with her decision. Fully expecting the worst, Jane told her team to pack up and they flew back to corporate. Jane told me, "A career without courage is limiting– how can you like the person in the mirror?"

The cost of courage

"If integrity is important to me, there is a price associated."
Harriet Seward

Often courage comes in the small everyday acts - making the right decision. Often the decisions we make early in our career set the tone and define our reputation for the rest of our career. The most difficult decisions affect not only our career and family, but also the people who depend on us.

Courage sometimes comes with a cost. Several interview participants told stories of doing the right thing early in their career when their children were small and the stakes were especially high. Taking a stand sometimes meant losing their jobs.

Bernie Hale, now a consultant, had just graduated from college and started his first job as a sales manager for a regional carrier. There was a legendary traffic manager who controlled large volumes of freight for a potential client. Bernie had a meeting with the traffic manager, who then asked his assistants to leave the room. He said, "Buy my car new tires and you'll get the freight."

Bernie said, "Pardon me sir?" He didn't think he had heard right. College hadn't prepared him for this. Bernie excused himself and returned to the office. He struggled for two days. It wasn't just him – the lives of 200 employees were in his hands. Was he so pure that he could make a decision that affected his co-workers and drivers?

Bernie says, "It turned my stomach to challenge them. People lose their jobs doing what is right – they answer to a higher calling." But where do you draw the line? This time it was tires, what would it be the next time - a car? It took all his courage to pick up the phone and refuse the offer. The traffic manager slammed down the phone. Bernie didn't go to his boss until after he had made the decision. There was a long pause. There was no praise but his boss stood behind him.

Bernie's decision cost his company a lot of freight. It affected the company's economic existence because the freight went to a direct competitor, the full trailers sitting on the lot next door. The employees couldn't understand why they weren't getting the business and Bernie couldn't explain.

Years later, the traffic manager retired and Bernie got the freight, needing all available capacity to handle it. Bernie is now semi-retired, but he vividly remembers that day, the black suit he was wearing and how he felt.

He says, "Everything that happens to you becomes a building block as you grow older. They are character builders making us better spouses, better parents and better leaders. That is the reward for doing what is right."

Is courage innate?

"Sometimes our fears can grip us so tightly
we are not able to act."
Harriett Seward

If courage comes with a cost, it must be its own reward - at the end of the day, liking the person in the mirror, being able to sleep at night; at the end of your career, looking back without fear that you let yourself down.

The most fascinating discussion in my character-centered leadership interview series came from the question, "Is courage an innate trait or can it be developed?" Olympians and business leaders alike wrestled with the answer. The final consensus was that courage is a combination of nature and nurture.

But developing courage in those you lead can be difficult, especially when people have mortgages, kids in school and community involvement. Many people are afraid for their jobs today. The press reports the raw numbers of lay-offs and unemployment statistics but not the anxiety, the holding of breath through each round of lay-offs. People are reluctant to take risks when they feel they are expendable at the first sign of economic downturn.

For some people, their whole identity is wrapped up in their job title, company name and salary. When they lose their job, they leave a big chunk of themselves behind. Developing an identity outside of work can help build courage - at the end of the day, you still get to go home to your family and life outside the office.

Others can't have courage because they are drowning in debt. They can't speak up or take a chance because they are living from paycheck to paycheck. Any interruption would bring financial ruin.

Sometimes, fear carries over from previous company experiences, but courage is innate in all of us and can be developed. You can create a culture of courage by encouraging your people to speak up in meetings and challenge the status quo.

Courage comes from commitment

"The many pressures of the marketplace can compromise an individual's values to do what is expedient. When people don't feel invested in the organization, they may not stand up for what is right. This works against people being true to their values."
Nancy Haslip

Courage comes from staying the course when it is uncomfortable or difficult. When there are 100 reasons to quit, you must have 101 reasons to stay. During the years it took to research and write this book, there were many times I wanted to give up. Friends and family questioned the marketability of the book and urged me to find a real job. But at each point of deep discouragement, someone always said, "What you are doing is important – you must not quit," giving me the fresh courage to last a bit longer.

Courage comes from digging down deep when you can't take one more step, when your finances, energy and emotional reserves are drained and you think there is nothing left.

Ken Wappel, CEO of the LTA group, remembers sitting on the grimy floor of a warehouse in the worst neighborhood of Patterson, NJ. Ken and his partner sat for hours drinking a six-pack of Heinekens, not knowing what to do, trying to figure out how to get out of trouble. At the business's three-year point, payables were higher than receivables and the other partners wanted out. Ken felt it was one thing to walk away with a break even, but another thing to fail. He couldn't quit the business without paying the people who had trusted them.

After reviewing existing accounts, Ken fired his non-profitable accounts and went to his good customers, explained they were in trouble and needed to raise their rates. To his amazement, they agreed and the company went from a negative to a positive cash flow. Today, LTA serves the top 25 retailers in the country.

Courage comes from strength

"Judo puts you in situations where you have to have courage. That builds the self-confidence to continue. Judo just builds strong people."
Sandy Bacher
Three-time Olympian, World Gold medalist women's wrestling

As a competitor, I've learned that it is impossible to maintain peak physical performance year round. Instead I follow a training schedule to reach a peak level of performance and conditioning right before critical competitions. During the off season when competition slows, I rest, rejuvenate and repair muscle and cartilage. This concept of peak conditioning also applies to our professional lives. We must take care of our physical selves to reach peak professional performance.

Often in judo competition, matches are won and lost in the last 30 seconds of stamina, determination and the will to win. In practice, we put our students through 30-second drills. We wait until the end of class when the players are exhausted, out of breath and soaked with sweat. We put them through two rounds of fighting and tell them to imagine they are fighting for the Gold at the Olympics. When 30 seconds remain on the clock, we call out, "30 seconds – all you've got!" Somehow, from somewhere deep inside, they find a new burst of strength and energy to win the match.

When you are mentally and physically drained and all you want is to give up, where do you find the stamina to endure? Where do you draw the strength to continue? What sustains you? "My strength is wearing low, but I have confidence everything that happens is for a reason. Some good comes out of everything," writes an anonymous reader.

Courage comes from having the physical stamina to withstand stress. It is difficult to act with courage when your body is worn down from anxiety, fatigued from fighting health problems, or when you can't think clearly from the after-effects of too much alcohol.

During periods of high pressure and demanding schedules, it is easy to bury our stress and anxiety in food. We fight back fatigue with rich restaurant meals. But unrelenting stress takes a heavy toll on our bodies, accelerating the aging process. How many times can you grab a quick bite at your desk, work late and fight traffic without it wearing down your body?

Too often we take our bodies for granted, neglecting to develop the physical body as we do our minds and professional skills. We know that physicality provides stress relief and increases energy levels. The discipline of a strong body gives us mental and emotional strength. To have continued courage, we must replenish our strength with adequate rest, good nutrition and exercise to relieve stress.

Work will always win out over fitness unless you make it a higher priority. When you put it on a back burner, fitness can become one more thing to feel guilty about. We need a healthy diet and a strong body to have the stamina for the second halves of our careers.

When we excuse ourselves from working toward fitness, saying there is no time, we also take away an important outlet for stress. To make fitness a habit, it is important to find the right activity for you – one that feels like play. Being fit then is not so much a chore as a time for socializing or precious time alone. With practice, the craving for fitness becomes a hunger as real as food.

"My running time this morning is just as important as my meetings and phone calls. Running is an 'A' priority because I've made it an 'A' priority," says Larry Mercer. "The connection between fitness and job performance is absolute. Fitness is part of self-esteem. It shows that you value your life. Physical fitness makes you clearer, more precise." You have one body. Take care of it.

Courage comes from confidence

"Courage and leadership are synonymous. Guide your people to do the right thing and protect unpopular acts of courage. You must have a covenant to protect and encourage in that path."
Fred Ball

You can develop courage in your own department by having courage yourself and expecting it in others, by letting the people you lead see your courage in your daily actions. Sometimes we must borrow courage from others to develop our own. In sharing your strength, your people will reflect your courage in their own decisions.

Courage comes from reaching a level of maturity; from being comfortable in your own skin and confident in your leadership, when you reach a point of trying to improve but are no longer trying to impress.

Courage comes with practice and past experiences – repetition and small successes build confidence. You can develop courage in the people you lead by giving them responsibility. Talk through both the risks and the value of what they are doing. Walk them through the tough decisions and protect them from political fallout. When your people make mistakes, stand behind them and give them the chance to make it right. As their confidence grows from each small success they will become braver.

Courage comes from facing the consequences. If you are so fearful of a negative outcome, you will not be able to act with courage. Ask yourself, "What is the worst thing that will happen if I act on my conviction? Can I face the possibility of being fired? Can I bear the consequences of marginalization and losing my power base?"

Then ask, "What is the worst thing that will happen if I don't?" Will you risk your reputation, become embittered, transfer to another department or leave the company?

Courage comes from heart

We tell our competitors that how you conduct yourself on the mat carries over to all parts of your life. We teach them to bow respectfully to their opponent, to fight hard, to accept wins and losses with equal measures of humility and grace. Sport, taught correctly, builds character.

When I took my coaching certification class, it was easy. Although I was new to coaching, I applied all the managerial principles I'd been using for years. Over the years, I've seen many naturally gifted athletes come and go. I'd rather coach a less talented, hard working athlete who has a clear mind and strong heart.

One of the privileges of being a coach is to watch athletes grow in confidence and courage with each competition. Often, it is hard to keep fighting. I ask my competitors, "How badly do you want it?" I push them hard in practice, demanding their best effort, praising and pushing in equal measures. "You have to believe it," I tell them when I see the doubt and fear in their eyes. As a coach, I've learned that techniques can be taught and courage can be developed. But it takes an athlete who is all heart to push past failure and disappointment, and stay in the game.

We coached a seven-year-old boy, Jonathan, with a blond crew-cut and big blue eyes. He was regularly beaten in practice by his partners. I told Jonathan, "You have to believe you can do it before you'll be able to throw him," but he became more timid, ending several practices in tears. Hoping to encourage him, Jonathan's father took him to a small, beginner's tournament. Our hearts sank when we saw his opponent bow onto the mat wearing a brown belt from another martial art.

The entire team sat on the side of the mat, cheering Jonathan on. We held our breath as he fought his heart out. To our amazement, Jonathan threw the brown belt for a full point, winning the match. He lost his second match, then came back to beat the brown belt again in the third match. He bowed off the mat to the cheers, hugs and back slapping congratulations of his teammates.

At the next practice, Jonathan was promoted to his yellow belt. With newfound confidence and determination, he started winning matches in practice and competition. About six months later, Jonathan was fighting a gold medal match. In the middle of the match, Jonathan spit his tooth out and handed it to the referee. He walked back to his starting line, while the referee watched dumb founded. The referee swallowed hard, put the tooth in his pocket, and re-started the match. Jonathan kept fighting, winning the match and the gold medal.

In business we sometimes face complex moral issues. Sports competition is more clear-cut; there is a winner and loser. If you do the right thing for your company, but get fired have you won or lost? Clearly there has been a high cost. But if you leave with your character intact you have a moral victory.

Courage comes from culture

"In World War II, fighter pilots were led on by other pilot's courage."
Mel Paisley

In the early 1990s at The Home Depot, an orientation video told the story of the courage Bernie Marcus and Arthur Blank displayed in starting the company after being fired from Handy Dan. The story was part of the folklore that made them our heroes and the core of Depot's strong corporate culture. When I joined the company, I spent 90 days traveling to the stores, learning the home improvement business and building relationships. Being a female director was a big deal back then. On my store visits, female associates would rush up to meet me and tell me how proud they were of my accomplishment.

I had been with Home Depot for four months when I attended my first storewide meeting. I did a lot of listening to the 300 plus store managers who had been like older brothers to me. I sat quietly at a divisional meeting as they discussed high turnover problems with the mostly female cashiers. They couldn't understand why the women were leaving. It was obvious to me that the women didn't think they had the same opportunities that were minting millionaires through the store manager development program.

One of the few women in the room, I listened as long as I could, then took the microphone as it passed around the room. Heart thudding, I made an impassioned, impromptu speech about giving the women the same opportunities and challenges in the management training program. "Work them as hard," I exhorted. "Expect as much, but give them the same opportunities." When I finished, there was a moment of total silence that stretched on forever. I stood there thinking, "I've blown it. I wonder if I can quietly pack my bags and catch the next flight home." The room erupted in applause and shouts of approval. Just when I started to breathe again, the room went silent. No one had noticed that Bernie had quietly slipped into the back of the room.

My heart sank as Bernie strode to the front of the room and snatched the microphone from my hand. I was sure to be fired and sent home in disgrace. "She's right," Bernie said, "Just because she's not standing next to you at the urinal, doesn't mean she can't do the job." I sank into my chair, weak with relief, as Bernie continued to lecture the store managers about opportunities for all associates. I learned a lesson about the courage of my convictions that day.

Courage comes from pushing past fear

"This is my life and my business. I don't want to end up knocking on the door of the homeless shelter, asking if they can spare a cot. I'm putting everything I have into this business. That is a little bit terrifying at times. I have to bear down and work through the fear."
Wendy Tarzian

Courage is not the absence of fear, but rather pushing forward in the face of that fear. For an athlete, the very worst thing is to know you gave your all and it was not enough. But maybe the very worst thing is to not give your all and always wonder what might have happened. Maybe the worst thing is to look back at the end of your career and be filled with regret over risks not taken.

To be a courageous leader you need to operate from your bedrock of beliefs. Courage comes from what you must do. From believing in something so strongly that you will do whatever it takes. From being who you are no matter where you are. We've all heard of top athletes using visualization to increase athletic performance. Jimmy Pedro, judo World Champion and three time Olympian took visualization a step further. "You have to believe it can happen before you are capable of becoming a champion," he says.

He not only pictured himself beating his opponents, he pictured what it would feel like, the goose bumps from standing on the medal stand, hearing our national anthem, feeling the weight of that heavy gold medal around his neck. Jimmy believed he could win the World Championships and made it a reality.

But back in the corporate world, sometimes in the time pressures and heat of work demands, we get in a hurry and make mistakes. We lose sight of our fundamental beliefs. Holding tight to your core values will keep you grounded.

A study on social courage showed that participants held more firmly to what they knew was the truth when they wrote it down. How strong is your commitment to living by your values?

In our unforgiving environment where even CEOs are shuffled every few years, you have to have something to hold onto. You have to be able to say, "This is who I am, this is what I believe, and this is what I stand for."

Show courage in the strength of your character

"Courage, bravery, valor – these words have been tied to the military, but they also refer to the inner battles raging within us."
John Ridley

The courage of character is old-fashioned stuff. It often comes out in crises - the small voice that says, "You are better than this," when you need a shower to wash away the unpleasantness of the day; when you question the person you've become and whether you much like being that person. This is who you are with the veneer stripped off.

As you think about your own life and career, is there an area where you need courage? You may have to dig down deep to find it. But with hard work, determination and commitment, it is possible. Because courage is in you, it shows in the strength of your character and the quality of your leadership. As courage becomes part of your core values, you will lead with both head and heart. And you will look back at the end of your career without regrets because you will have given it your all.

Most of us are never tested in a dramatic fashion. We don't represent our country at the Olympics. We don't ever have to make those "you bet your career" type of decisions. Many of us have not faced the great challenges that strengthen our resolve. But practicing courage in the small moments and everyday acts and decisions prepares you for the time you will have to face down your fear.

Chapter Four

Leadership Questions

- Does courage have a place in today's corporate environment?

- Can you give me an example of courage in the workplace?

- Have you ever faced fear in your career?

- Is courage an innate trait or can it be developed?

- How do you develop courage in those you lead?

Chapter Five

Making The Most Contribution

Winter 1998

"The principle of maximum efficiency, whether applied to the art of attack and defense or to refining and perfecting daily life, demands, above all, that there be order and harmony among people. This can be realized only through mutual aid and concession. The result is mutual welfare and benefit. The final aim of judo practice is to inculcate respect for the principles of maximum efficiency and mutual welfare and benefit."
Jigoro Kano, founder of Kodakan Judo

In January, my judo teammates and I began training in earnest, preparing for our first regional tournament of the year. I was hesitant in practice, afraid to take falls, my back as fragile as glass. When the time came to test for my green belt, I declined. Pain prevented me from training all out, stiffness in my lower back kept me from executing the more physical throws. I decided to wait until summer to test.

Legend has it that the belt ranking system originated from years of use. As a person began to practice judo, their white belt would turn yellow with sweat, then become stained green with grass stains from ground work. Repeated practice would turn the belt brown with bloodstains and finally black with years of practice and wear. Today, black belt judo players wear their oldest belts, frayed white around the edges, showing the years of work and training. Students are told to never wash their belts; to do so will wash out the years of knowledge the belt stores.

On promotion night, the weekend before the tournament, I watched the successful students go to the front of the line. Sensei praised each student's progress and testing success as he untied their old belt and tied on the higher-ranking belt. Each player who outranked the newly promoted student threw them to celebrate their accomplishment.

I was surprised when sensei called me to the front of the line. As he untied my orange belt and tied on a crisp green belt, he told the class of my courage to return to the mat. I certainly didn't feel courageous or that I deserved the green belt. But when I took my celebratory falls, I wasn't thrown as many times. I was moving up in rank.

At the tournament that weekend, I stood at the side of the mat before each match, trembling with fear and adrenalin. The injury, still fresh in my mind, made me fearful to risk turning into throws, pain prevented me from bridging out of pins. I was humiliatingly defeated, my green belt still stiff with newness. I sat watching the women in my division fight for the Gold, struck by their beauty of motion and grace, their flexibility and speed.

I wasn't only fighting the injury, but fighting the clock, not knowing the next year if I would still be competing. Already I had watched athletes come and go in judo. I had witnessed athletes burn out, get injured and drop out.

Charlie Hooks, an older referee with gray-green eyes set deep in a coffee colored face, took me aside. He walked with a pronounced limp, knees worn out from decades of judo. Referees are bound by a strict code of conduct during tournaments. They are not allowed to fraternize with the players, to avoid charges of favoritism, much less coach them. But Charlie saw my desolation and risked demotion to help. He took me aside and coached me because he saw I needed coaching and his encouragement to stay in the sport.

The torn ligaments in my back stitched back together slowly, despite my willing the healing to hurry. Non-practice nights were spent training with a personal trainer to strengthen supporting muscles or in massage therapy. Each visit to my orthopedic surgeon and chiropractor yielded another lecture to find a new sport, one less wearing on my body.

My faithful practice partner, Shelia went through a traumatic divorce and had to drop out. Months went by without a suitable practice partner. But as my back mended, my fighting spirit returned - the drive to win the Gold returned. I began winning more matches.

At work I was restless. I sat in my office in the late afternoon, day dreaming about the next competition, about having more time to train, travel and compete. I sat at my desk, listlessly pushing around paper, wondering if I could do this for the next twenty years.

I sat through every boring meeting, every babble-speak session with the consultants, listening to their meaningless, empty words with an un-named urgency. I circled vacation and holidays on my monthly planner. I had always been a workaholic, but my heart was no longer in it.

I felt lucky to have a good job with a solid company, and a strong mission. Why wasn't it enough? Surface problems of a personality conflict with a new boss and political clashes over the department's direction seemed unimportant. They were merely symptomatic of a larger restlessness, a rising chord of dissatisfaction. I felt like my life was slipping through my fingers like water. I was being called, but to what?

In May I was downsized, set free to live an athlete's life. In pushing me out, my boss did me a great favor. I could not have left the steady paycheck nest. Now I was free to focus on training and competing. Free to find my calling. What would it be?

This newfound freedom to choose was heady stuff - something I had not been raised to seek out. My parents didn't expect to find fulfillment in their work. They worked night and day to pay the mortgage, feed six kids and keep us in clothes and shoes. Their day started at 5:30 a.m. when my dad left for work. He spent the day welding in an un-air-conditioned shop, then came home to work in the vegetable garden until dark. Mom took care of six kids and babysat for extra money. Every night she packed my dad's metal lunchbox, baking a cake that lasted only a day. Every morning she filled his thermos with hot coffee. They struggled through the lean years when the union called the men out on strike, suffering the small town embarrassment of food stamps and free school lunches.

To survive the lean years, my parents raised an enormous garden. It provided fresh vegetables to stretch every meal in the summer. Weeks spent working in a steamy, hot kitchen canning and preserving meant produce for winter. They also raised rabbits and kept them well cared for with alfalfa pellets and fresh water, clean cages, and wooden box shelters until it was their time to feed the family.

I helped my dad slaughter the rabbits in the garage. He held them upside down by their feet, smoothing their fur, talking to them in a soothing tone until the terror was gone from their eyes. He killed them instantly with a quick chop to the neck and cut off the head to let the blood flow. I helped him skin the carcasses, holding onto their feet as he pulled the fur over the head. When he cut open the stomach, the entrails sent an acrid smell steaming into the air.

While my parents' jobs paid the bills, they found their fulfillment in their church and in raising six successful kids. Who was I to expect more than a paycheck for my time at the office?

I had spent 18 years, my daughter's lifetime, in the logistics profession. I had just begun taking part-time college classes, when I discovered I was pregnant. When I held my newborn daughter in my arms - porcelain pink with impossibly long eyelashes - I promised she wouldn't grow up in poverty. I swallowed my pride and moved back home with my parents. For seven years, I worked full time, raised my daughter and went to school. Two semesters from graduation, I hit a wall. Exhausted, out of money and burned out, I was ready to quit.

My advisor urged me to talk to Dr. Bernard LaLonde, the head of the transportation and logistics program at The Ohio State University. A scrawny student in ragged blue jeans, I sat in awe in front of LaLonde, an icon in the industry.

I promised, "If you will help me apply for scholarships to graduate, I will give back and make a contribution to logistics." My grades were good enough, and with Dr. LaLonde's recommendations, the scholarship money starting flowing.

But there was a catch. As I accepted the scholarships, I had to give an acceptance speech. In my senior year, I started leading a double life; scruffy student by day, eating popcorn and soup, wearing tee shirts and tennis shoes; and sleek speaker by night. I had one navy suit, found on the clearance rack of an upscale department store. The suit was too good for me - when I took it to the cash register, the clerk asked me suspiciously, "Did you switch the price tags?" Throughout my senior year I wore my one good suit and sensible pumps, accepting awards and making speeches to logistics leaders old enough to be my father.

With LaLonde's help, I graduated and launched a successful career in logistics. I kept my promise to give back to the profession, serving in logistics associations, mentoring young men and women. I bought a book on charting your life goals and mapped out goals that seemed impossible to reach.

Ten years later, in the late Indian summer of 1998, downsized and aimless, I found my goals journal again. In re-reading those early ambitions, I realized I had actually reached all of my financial and professional goals. Why then, was I so unfulfilled?

I went through the motions of executive outplacement, testing and group discussions, not sure where I would end up. One afternoon, another outplacement participant stopped me in the hallway. "When you talk about returning to corporate, you're all business," he said. "But when you talk about sharing your message, your face lights up, your eyes become alive."

My choice - my path - became clear, but I was a reluctant entrepreneur. For many people, starting their own business is a life-long dream. For me, it was a nightmare riddled with risk. I bore the scars of my ex-husband's business failure that brought us one house payment away from bankruptcy. My daughter, with the wisdom of her teenage years, said, "But mom, if you want to teach people how to lead with courage, you have to show courage yourself."

I began the process of retooling and retraining, of repackaging myself for a new career. It is closer to the truth to admit that I retreated. I needed time to determine if I had the courage to take the entrepreneurial leap. I walked away from corporate, looking over my shoulder at opportunity as it dropped off the horizon. Two closets of suits hung in their plastic bags, waiting patiently. My briefcase gathered dust as I pushed the pause button.

I missed being around business people who wore their power lightly and made tough decisions with easy grace. In the stillness of the early morning I sat at my kitchen table and drank coffee, reading business magazines about a world I had lost.

All I had was the message that I wasn't sure anyone would want to hear and the sense that time was running out. Would people respond to a message that was real and raw? I didn't know. But I felt I had something to say that would change people's lives in a small way.

At this point, I knew my logistics career didn't matter anymore; that I had to find meaning beyond building wealth, buying another luxury car or a bigger house. I had a deep longing to do work that mattered; that made a difference in people's lives. I looked at all my material possessions and said, "This is enough." I was ready to trade stuff for the chance to do something significant.

The search for significance

"My father told me to choose a career for the money and doing what is in my heart could be a hobby. But that's not true. There is so little time. You spend 90% of your life not where your heart is. I will tell my children to do something they love."
Susan Uramoto

As I set out to answer my call, I found that I was not the only one searching. My pastor recommended a slim book, *Half Time*, written by Bob Buford. *Half Time* promised that the second half of my life could be better, more rewarding, than my first half. It showed how I could use my education and professional experience to move from success to significance. I read and re-read each chapter, underlining and highlighting, making notes in the margin until the book was ragged with wear.

In *Half Time*, Buford discusses how we spend the first half of our lives gaining, earning and learning. We become well educated, build a career and accumulate wealth and the trappings of success. Many of us are knocked down during the long and costly climb: divorce, estrangement from our children, guilt, loneliness, pain and disappointment. Buford writes of the success panic that hits when we realize we've reached all of our goals and begin to question, "How much is enough?" He argues that we can have a midlife crisis and enjoy a second half that is productive and fulfilling, one that builds on all we have invested in the first half of our lives.

Men caught in midlife crisis are not the only ones searching for significance. *Fast Company's* Harriett Rubin writes, "…for many businesswomen today, the magic "S" word has shifted meaning. They see the work of making life (S for significance) as an antidote to the emptiness that comes with simply making a living (S for success).

Significance means doing work you are called to do rather than work you want to do or work that merely pays well. It means following a vocation rather than performing a job."[1]

Every career has its ups and downs. We've all had experiences of unrelenting stress or working under a dislikable boss. During this tight job market, we don't have a choice but to grit our teeth and hang on until the economy improves. Most of us can't afford to "follow our bliss," to trade our vocation for our avocation. Still we wonder, is it possible to do important work on and off the job? Can we find fresh meaning in our career by passing down our hard won wisdom to the next generation?

The search to serve

"Giving back is the manifestation of a grateful heart."
Jon Ridley

With the leading edge of the baby boomers at age 55, a large portion of them are entering their "pre-retirement" years. Nearly 20% of the nation's workers will be 55 years old or older by 2015, up from 13% today, according to the Bureau of Labor Statistics.[2] This year, for the first time, the number of workers over 40 will surpass those under 40.[3]

This aging workforce, rich in experience and institutional knowledge, has been largely untapped. Though some companies have adopted phased retirement to retain the company history, during downsizing, pre-retirees are often the first to be offered a buy-out package.

Increasingly, these seasoned, professional managers bump into age discrimination. As a society we don't honor the wisdom that comes from experience. AARP held a contest to find the best employers for workers over 50. They mailed invitations to 10,000 companies but only 14 responded.[4]

Energetic boomers who are not content to coast until retirement are looking for an outlet for their energy, vitality and intellect. I recently talked to a man in his mid-50s, successful, stable and financially secure. He had accumulated enough wealth to retire. "But retire to what?" he asked. "As everyone introduced themselves at a civic club breakfast meeting this week, I realized I couldn't introduce myself in any context other than work. If I retire, I know the people whom I spend so much time with today won't visit me."

He paused, letting the realization soak in. "So many of us don't have the courage to do something significant. I'm ready to do something significant with my life," he concluded.

At the same time we are retiring at an earlier age, we are staying younger longer and living healthier lives. What will we do with two or even three decades after retirement? How much golf can we play?

We've all heard stories of hard charging executives who put off a lifetime of leisure until retirement, only to drop dead less than a year later. We have learned that our lives must have meaning and purpose; that we must have a reason to keep living.

As boomers are forced into early retirement, they look beyond the traditional functions of serving on corporate or charity boards or teaching business classes. They are searching for ways to share their time, energy and experience to make a difference. As we mature in our professional and personal life, we long to make a larger contribution, to leave our mark. When we reach a level of success, we want to share our good fortune. And as we suffer the bumps and bruises of life, we want to share our life lessons, to help others avoid our mistakes.

Values vs. pleasure

"Lots of people have voids in their life – they don't know where to turn."
Angela Monroe

As we get older, we face our own mortality. When Dr. Steven Reiss faced death while awaiting a liver transplant, he began to question the Pleasure Principle, which says that we are motivated to maximize pleasure and minimize pain."[5]

He asked over 6,000 people which values are most significant in motivating their behavior and contributing to their happiness. Reiss found that values, not pleasure, are what bring true happiness and that everybody has the potential to live in accordance with their values.[6]

Reiss argues that "Values-based happiness is a sense that our lives have meaning and fulfill some larger purpose. It represents a spiritual source of satisfaction, stemming from our deeper purpose and values."[7]

"When the world is crumbling around you and you don't agree with the forces that drive change, you must be anchored to your values," says Tim Duffy. The mood of the country changed dramatically after 9/11. We saw each other at our best, our most unselfish and heroic. We put politics aside and grieved at a national loss not felt since the JFK assassination. In the weeks that followed, fear and foreboding produced short-term change. We focused on our most urgent priorities and common vulnerability. We stood united, trusting in God and country.

Gradually we realized we had to move forward, to go on with our lives or remain paralyzed with fear. Now we shrug off almost weekly warnings of new attacks.

As the smoke and somberness of the times drifted away from the void that used to be the twin towers, many of us sought longer lasting change. Those who were spared on 9/11 through fate, or grace or happenstance have a chance to do something significant with their lives. So do you. We learned from 9/11 that life is too short not to do something important.

As Rabbi Harold S. Kushner writes of a young person dying too soon, "We have to do something so that this person we loved and lost will not have died in vain. Whether it be a call for new laws or for more medical research, we need to reassure ourselves that something good can come out of the tragedy. We can just barely accept the fact that good people die too soon. It is too much for us to think that their lives may have been wasted."[8]

The search for significance spans several generations. USA Today reports that this year's college graduates are turning to volunteer work in droves. Teach for America, which recruits recent graduates to teach in a public or rural school received 14,000 applications, nearly triple last year's 4,946 applicants. Ameri-Corps, a national service program saw a 75% increase in online applications from graduating seniors this year.[9]

Making quiet contributions

"Winning isn't everything. Having a medal around your neck doesn't make you a success. I have more respect for those who have worked hard for years, but have always been number two, always the alternate for the Olympic team. The character within you is more important."
Sandy Bacher,
Three-time Judo Olympian and World Gold medalist, women's wrestling

Keith Nakasone made the Olympic team in 1979, the same year the Soviet Union invaded Afghanistan. The United States, along with most Western Countries, boycotted the 1980 Olympics to apply international pressure on the Soviets.

Keith stayed home, doing what his country called on him to do. But missing the Olympics took away his lifetime dream. "Boycotting the Olympics had a negative impact on my life. All the time I had invested, all the money – it had major repercussions in my life," he says. "I was very angry. I went into a shell. I put my judo gear into a duffel bag and didn't take it out for four years. That was my way of coping with the disappointment."

Later Keith realized that other players suffered because of his immaturity. Now a college coach at San Jose in California, he has built a successful collegiate judo program and coached Sandy Bacher to three Olympic teams. Keith regrets not sharing his talents during his years of withdrawal.

"What could I have given back to the sport and to these college kids during those years?" he asks. "Many athletes feel their sport owes them something. That is not true. We owe our sport everything."

Most of us are not Olympians or CEOs. We are ordinary businessmen and women. But we each have a platform, which is both a privilege and responsibility.

As a professional speaker, I have a platform. About a year ago I was speaking to a business group when the room became very, very quiet. They were really with me, taking the message and applying it to their lives. It scared me. Because, in that moment, I realized there was an opportunity for great good or great harm.

Sometimes people apply my message in ways that I would not have dreamed. Once, I spoke to a group of professional women. A pregnant woman within weeks of delivering her baby, came up after the presentation and told me the message was specifically for her. I thought I was talking about courage in a corporate setting, but can you imagine a situation that requires more courage than putting your life on the line to give birth to a new life?

As a referee, when I wear that black jacket of absolute authority, I have a platform. I have to referee that 5-year-old white belt just as fairly and impartially as the elite athlete fighting for a national championship. Someday, that 5-year-old white belt may grow up to become an Olympian.

You have a platform - in your leadership role at work, in your activity in the community. You have a platform in your role as a parent and spouse. You have a privilege and responsibility to lead with honor and use your platform for great good.

Kushner asks, "Can one ordinary person really change things? Can we, in our anonymity, affect history? Rarely we can, by what we do alone, move mountains and make a difference. But by being good people and doing good things, we can, as members of a community dedicated to goodness, change the world. We can matter."[10]

What will inspire you?

"What I am going to do with Lou is a fearful thing. I never thought I would be part of the Olympics. After that experience, I don't have to prove myself anymore. I have reached the highest point of my life. I have found a new latitude to do something grand with my life. The Olympic high is still there. It's still in me. I don't ever want to lose that feeling. Now I need to find a big goal. The Olympics made me a different person. Where it takes me from here, I don't know. I have to sit back and figure out what I want to do now. I need more than a job and money. The Olympic experience was so fulfilling – what will fulfill me again?"
Lou Moyerman
Team Leader for the 2000 Sydney Olympic Judo Team

Like Lou, many of us are searching for a larger sense of service. We dabble in various volunteer activities, we write checks to charity. We look for a cause we can champion, for something beyond ourselves that we can believe in and commit to with our whole heart.

The search for significance can come from an event so positive it transforms your life. Sometimes our success inspires us to use our platform and talents to create something bigger and more lasting than ourselves.

You may be hearing a call to change careers, to step off the fast track and devote yourself more to family or volunteer work. We take the long view when we feel a commitment to those who come after us; our children, our children's children.   We are willing to make sacrifices today for a greater good tomorrow. We work to build things that endure, to leave a legacy.

Or perhaps you feel you can make a larger impact where you serve today. You've reached a point of success, name recognition and influence in your field where you can make the greatest contribution from your existing platform.   Buford writes, "What we become in the second half has already been invested during the first; it is not going to come out of the blue. I am the same me I was in the first half, only applied to a different venue."[11]

Serving those who need you the most

"When I was in the fifth grade I told my Grandpa that I was going to college. He said, "That's a big word for a small girl." I come from a long line of losers. I wanted to break the chain – I always knew I would go to college,"
Virginia Gray

Who needs you the most? How can you find out where you are needed most? Sometimes people are put into your path.

Misty Haskins worked as my intern during her senior year of high school. She was the second in an extended family of almost 40 relatives to graduate from high school, and the first in her family to attempt college.   When Misty talked about going to college tears welled up in her eyes – college seemed like an impossible dream. Sensei and I supported and encouraged Misty through three years of college. When we danced at her wedding, right before her college graduation, we knew our mentoring role had ended. Misty was going to make it.

Recently, I refused to serve on a mentoring program for young professional women.   The mentoring program was admirable, worthy and necessary. But I am needed far more here in Kentucky with its career ending combination of poverty, teen pregnancy and high school dropouts. I am needed to be a daily, visible role model for teenage girls like Misty. Serving where you are needed most means saying no to worthy causes that take you away from making the greatest impact.

In your search for significance, never forget that family must come first. Some people get mixed up; they put serving their church or community above family. Our first obligation is to raise our children in a stable, loving home that gives them a solid grounding in values. Our most important life role is parenting.

Ray Dunmeyer is a three-time Judo Para-Olympian. He says, "From my father, I learned you must pay your debts. I overheard my father crying when he learned I had glaucoma. He asked the doctors, "Can you take one of my eyes so my son can see?"

In judo practice and regular competition, visually impaired players compete against sighted athletes. They fight under the same Olympic rules with only a few minor modifications to safely start and stop the match. Dunmeyer recounts, "When I missed judo practice because I couldn't pay, my coach asked why I wasn't coming. I was embarrassed to admit I didn't have the money."

He told me, "You can come to practice, but you must pay me back. Your obligation to me is to train as hard as you can – then find 10 other people in need and help them." Ray went on to represent the United States as a three-time Para-Olympian. Today he is an executive for UPS and coaches his own judo club.

Growing up, I had early exposure to the concept of giving back. My mother led a weekly Bible study in our home. I was too young to remember any more than the ladies sipping hot black coffee in delicate china cups as they balanced matching saucers of yellow cake with chocolate frosting. Teaching that weekly Bible study and learning sign language so she could translate Sunday sermons to the deaf was my mother's way of giving back.

What is your obligation? How committed are you to giving back? I've often been criticized for the 10 to 20 hours a week I volunteer coaching and refereeing judo. I've been advised to give up my sport so I can put more hours into writing, building the business or simply relaxing.

But neither my book nor my business makes sense without the judo. I've made a commitment to my players, and I don't allow anything to get in the way of practice. As difficult as it is to stop working and drive to practice, once I'm absorbed in the players' progress, it's worth it. With each practice I make a visible, measurable difference in those children's lives.

There are valuable lessons to be learned from sports. After each tournament, we give out special awards to recognize individual successes: the fastest throw, the best fighting spirit, the most courage, most improved technique. As coaches, we recognize that not everyone can be a great athlete or win a medal. But each competitor can show improvement, fight hard and make a contribution to the club.

One night we had an extra award for best judo spirit. We left the definition intentionally vague and asked the parents watching practice to decide on the recipient. That night, all of the kids fought their hearts out, trying to win the award. At the end of practice we played "Duck, Duck Goose". In this game, the child who is "it" chases another around a large circle of kids lying on their stomach in pairs. The child being chased dives onto his stomach beside two children, forcing the third to jump up and run.

The kids were having fun until Griffin; the youngest and smallest at age four, became "it." He had a tough time catching the larger, faster kids. Griffin was "it" for five long rounds. We watched with growing dismay, and were about to stop the game. Suddenly, Jonathan, who was being chased, doubled over with a leg cramp. He began limping, barely able to hobble. With fresh energy, Griffin ran faster and tagged him. At the end of class, the parents voted unanimously to give the best judo spirit award to Jonathan - who skipped out of practice, faked leg cramp forgotten.

One life's difference

"Anne Marie was a ten-year-old little fat girl in my judo class back in the early 1970s. Twenty years later she called me. She and her brother had been trying to find me for years. She had a child with a mental disability. She said, "You have been an inspiration to me and my brother for 20 years. Whenever times are tough, I think, what would sensei do, what would sensei say? He would never give up." She wanted to thank me for giving her a creed to live her life by. I was crying; I couldn't wait to hang up the phone so I could really sob. You never know the impact you have on people's lives."
George Harris, 1964 Olympian

As thankful as we are for our naturally gifted athletes in judo, our primary responsibility is to develop the timid, the weak and the uncoordinated player. We invest years of training and developing the confidence of young athletes that carries over to all parts of their lives.

Inevitably, there comes a time when they no longer need us. We lose many to the better-funded, high visibility big sports. As hard as it is, we let them go because we have done our job. In a small way, we have prepared them for life by firming up their foundation.

We try hard not to play favorites, but for several years it was obvious to everyone that Chad was a favorite. Chad was always growing too fast for his physical coordination to catch up. He wasn't our best athlete or our most successful competitor, but Chad was always the first on the mat and the last to bow off. One night driving home after competition, Chad told us he had decided to become an astronaut when he grew up. He would become the first judo black belt in space – he reasoned that sensei would be ready to retire, and Chad would take over teaching the class. We didn't have the heart to tell him our small Kentucky town was an unlikely place for a space program.

Build on your talents

"My brother got beaten up on the playground, but he is still a champion. I was better in judo and became an Olympian. He became an attorney – we are both champions in our hearts. You can become #1 in many things – each has special skills and talents. Whatever you are good at, you must
come back and help others."
Grace Jividen-Chapman, 1992 Olympian

What will you do with your great gifts? What do you do so naturally and effortlessly that you take it for granted? Have you found yourself questioning in the stillness of early morning, or lain awake at night seeking answers? Have you wondered how you can build on your unique talents, your palm pilot of business contacts, your education and experience to make a lasting contribution?

The first part of hearing and answering our call is to tone down the noise and frenetic activity of everyday life. I could not have made the leap to change my career and change my life without in-depth introspection. Without the time to think and question, to read and reflect, I would have kept rushing through my daily routine. Too often we don't pause before the big decisions. We feel compelled to keep going, to do more, run faster like a hamster on a wheel.

What will it take you to slow down? My friend is a success story. She completed her teaching degree while pregnant with twins, so big with baby she couldn't fit into a desk. Ten years ago she switched careers and became an insurance agent.

Today she is a top producer, winning sales trips to exotic locales. She makes more money and has more of what we've always considered success than we ever could have imagined.

Last summer she sent me a sad email, "I have been a little heartsick lately; I have no time for anything. I am depressed and sorry that I feel heartsick. I want to deny that I feel this way. It seems awful to have everything you've always wanted and then to feel heartsick. I just feel downtrodden."

When her husband was in a car accident, everything stopped except a flurry of tests and medical specialists. Dan was unable to walk for weeks and she dropped everything to nurse him to recovery. He jokes that it took the accident to get her to come home from work. The accident and subsequent down time helped re-align her priorities and put the pressures of work into perspective.

Each choice we make takes us either closer or farther away from our purpose. To gain perspective, we must distance ourselves from daily work demands, family and home responsibilities. Understanding what you value takes quiet and time to think.

Growing up, we had more time to rest, to eat meals with family and friends. We still need time to clear our minds, to step back from the hurried bustle of everyday life, to reflect on the important. In our modern society, it is difficult to simply sit still and think. I've found that my best thinking comes during light activity such as walking, gardening, or even driving with the radio off. Others prefer to pray or meditate.

Identifying your major influences

"I am who I am because a whole lot of people invested in me."
Harriett Seward

There are many good books on clarifying your values and purpose. Juanelle Teague, of People Plus, a consultant and career coach, has a system I consider one of the most effective.[12] She begins by asking the following questions about your personal relationships and important mentors. These relationships could be with a parent, grandparent, a teacher or coach, sibling or friend.

Think about your key relationships and ask these questions:

- What relationship has made the most positive impact on your life? Why?
- What relationship has made the most negative impact on your life? Why?

- Who has been your most important role model? Why?
- How have these relationships affected your belief system?
- Who have been your master mentors?
- How have they affected your life?
- How have they affected your belief system? How are you different from them?

Teague believes we experience multiple turning points in our lives that shape our values and beliefs. These turning points, negative or positive, are a learning process, resulting in greater strength of character and wisdom. Teague's research has found that most people experience six turning points: as a young child (often this will be our earliest memory) as a pre-teen, during the turbulent teenage years, and as a young professional, intent on achieving and acquiring.[13] However, the most critical turning point occurs between 35 and 45 years of age and centers around failure in career, marriage or health. This is when we begin to question.

Your six turning points:

The year of each turning point.
- Your age?
- Describe the event
- Who was involved?
- What was the high point of this event?
- What was the low point of this event?
- What was the message you received about yourself or others?
- What was the impact on your personal growth?
- What life skills and knowledge did you gain?
- What character strength did you develop?
- What wisdom did you acquire?
- How was your response different from that of an average person?
- What innate ability helped you through this event?
- What did you enjoy from the experience?
- What gift have you gained from the experience?

When you summarize the life skills and the character strength and wisdom you developed at each of the turning points, you will have clarity on your call. You will be able to determine where you are needed most and what you must do to find significance.

Tom Koentop has worked in outplacement for many years. "A woman I worked with wanted to do something important with her life, but she would not lower her lifestyle to $50k from $100k. The call was not strong enough. She struggled between having an impact on people's lives and having dollars. Making a change doesn't happen often or easily. People have house and car payments. They have debt. They don't take the time to re-examine life and discover the mission of their life beyond dollars," he says.

Sometimes we fear that answering the call will make us a different person. Buford writes, "I used to think that if I ever said a complete yes to Christ, I would become a completely different person – that I would wear polyester and drive used cars, or ride a donkey in an AIDS-infested third world country doing things I had never enjoyed doing. I was relieved to discover that God does not waste what he has built."[14]

Others are simply unwilling to make the sacrifices. They allow their desire to make a good living to override their need for fulfillment.

Making the most contribution

Have you ever wanted something so badly it made your teeth ache? I wanted to wear a USA patch on the back of my uniform, to represent my country at the U.S. Open Judo Championships. I knew I didn't have the athletic gifts of my opponents, nor their skill or strength. Instead, I took everything that had helped me in my professional career and applied it to becoming an athlete.

I cross-trained six days a week, running and weight training, attended judo camps, always the oldest player on the mat. I drove long distances to Georgia and Indiana to study with different coaches. In Indiana, I trained with Holly, a sturdy athlete with long red hair bound up in a single braid down her back and a brown belt. A bronze medallist in Junior Olympics, Holly had strength and stamina. She worked two jobs and trained every night, putting a strain on her young marriage. When her husband asked her to choose him or judo, she chose her sport, although her brown eyes filled with tears. We spent the summer counting every calorie, running in the coolness of early mornings, each afternoon filled with mat techniques, working in extra evening practices with the club.

I spent a solid year of judo training, traveling and competing. But judo athletes peak in their twenties. The clock doesn't lie and time runs out. I learned that it is not enough to dream about a gold medal. It was not even enough to want it so badly your teeth ached.

I attended a training camp in Miami. I trained hard all week and was beaten by players half my age. At the end of the week, I sat outside, nursing my aches and bruises. Irwin Cohen, 1972 Olympian and 1992 Olympic coach came and sat beside me. He said, "You need to retire. You are going to get hurt. These young players are on their way to becoming an Olympian – they don't care if they throw you on your head or break your arm."

I felt the warm Miami breeze against my face. I looked into his eyes. They were kind. He continued, taking away my dream, "You started judo too late to become a national champion. Become a good referee instead – we need them." I knew he had my best interests at heart. I nodded in agreement. I didn't trust myself to speak.

I took his advice. I gave up my dream of the USA patch and faced the truth that my competitive career was over. After I retired from competition, all of the pressure came off at practice - judo became like play again.

I remembered the referee who coached and encouraged me when my back was as fragile as glass. I thought, "I can be a referee like Charlie."

I realized I could make a larger contribution to my sport by being a good referee. I could help the athletes learn by applying the rules fairly and impartially. Early in my judo career, I trained and thought like a competitor – it was all about me. Now, a national referee, I quietly encourage the athletes who fight their hearts out with great courage, but lose. They sit afterwards, alone, desolate, defeated. It is only a murmur passed quietly and quickly as we pass in the hall, no more than a "you fought well today" comment. I hope it helps. I think of Charlie.

Chapter Five

Leadership Questions

- What is the most important lesson you have learned?

- Do people expect a sense of doing something important and lasting from their work today?

- What is your life's work?

- What motivates you to give back? What are the rewards?

- What lessons will you pass down?

Chapter Six

The Lost Art Of Loyalty

A decade of downsizing

"Our parents went to work in the morning and stayed for life."
Fran Chargar, executive recruiter

Our parents spent most of their careers with one company. We baby boomers, on the other hand, have become veterans of lay-offs, bracing ourselves for yet another round of cuts. A 2000 study by Lee Hecht Harrison found 78% of baby boomers anticipated their organization's downsizing and fully 57% weren't surprised to be among those laid off. We've not only become accustomed to downsizing, we're adept at reading the writing on the walls and bear the battle scars to prove it.

The corporate world has changed since the days of life-long employment and men in gray flannel suits. In the early 1980s, we would watch the television news of blue-collar lay-offs. Those poor families, we'd think, smug in our education and white-collar work. In the late 1980s, *Re-engineering the Corporation,* by co-authors Hammer and Champy democratized lay-offs.

I first noticed the effect of downsizing when building my managerial team at The Home Depot in the early 1990s. In those days, Depot hired one associate out of 100 applicants, and I read a lot of resumes, trying to match talent and personality to the company culture.

I was struck by the similarity of resumes that crossed my desk. A man, in his mid 40's had been with his company for 20 years, progressing slowly but steadily. Suddenly he was downsized. Within two to four years, he had jumped from Company A to Company B, and was now sending his resume to me. In our interviews, these men sounded bewildered and bitter. They didn't understand what had happened.

Executive recruiter, Ellen Martin says, "Men more often than women become devastated by lay-offs because it takes away their self worth and sense of identity. They never forget the taste of being let go and never want to be in that position again."

Today, a decade of downsizing has taken a heavy toll. Many people feel betrayed and abandoned – their commitment to the organization has been replaced by fatigue, cynicism and mistrust. We no longer think of organizations as being benevolent.

The aftermath of an era of lay-offs has led to individualism and a sense of "I'd better get mine because the next rung of the corporate ladder is crumbling." Those who have been through multiple downsizings don't want to depend on the organization for security and the good life with all its trappings - the executive home and country club membership. They want to depend on themselves.

A look back at loyalty

"The greed-is-good mentality assassinated a large percentage of the workforce instead of just sucking out the cellulite."
Jim McCallie

The first rounds of lay-offs in the deep recession of the early 1990s were for economic survival. 78% of cuts in 1994 were driven by financial difficulties.[1] But lay-offs soon became fashionable as each announcement of cuts was quickly followed by a surge in share prices. CEOs competed to see which company could cut deeper, taking out layers of fat, sometimes cutting deep into muscle and bone.

Even after the economic recovery, lay-offs continued. There were publicly announced lay-offs of 700,000 people in the white hot economy of 1999.[2]

Before the recession in 2000, according to *Fast Company* magazine, employers cut 1.2 million workers, ending the year with the highest number of lay-offs since the Bureau of Labor Statistics resumed calculating them in 1995.[3] In 2000, only 21% of cuts were caused by financial difficulties as companies continued to realign their workforce to adapt to changes in technology, mergers and global competition.[4] 43% of U.S. based companies that have downsized in the past three years told Lee Hecht Harrison they anticipate another downsizing before 2003.[5]

Downsizing is no longer an exclusively American business practice. Managers in 18 countries agreed that widespread corporate downsizing had become common.[6]

Uncounted costs of lay-offs

"It takes away from a team when people are trying to survive downsizing. Those who have been with the company for 25 years could lose their jobs. It is very traumatic."
Daisy Ramirez

During a recession, companies use downsizing to achieve quarterly or annual goals and temporarily prop up share price. But we have learned that poorly thought-out and executed lay-offs result in lowered productivity, morale and mistrust. As *Fast Company* writes, "In those glib phrases of the day, "You'll get more for less" and a "win-win situation." Well, maybe. Lay-offs often don't deliver the promised quick fix. Instead, you may get burned out managers, angry workers, quality losses under the guise of productivity gains and bad service that alienates customers. In other words, you could get less for less and a lose-lose situation."[7]

63% of those polled by Lee Hecht Harrison said morale was lower and 50% said trust in management had been reduced after lay-offs. [8]

Low morale leads to higher absenteeism as people look for other work or can't shake off their lethargy to make it to the office. People who mistrust management won't raise their hand to offer ideas or take risks when the danger seems more real than the rewards.

The uncertainty of any future beyond next week's paycheck dramatically drops productivity. Fear and stress cause people to act out of character. They will expend enormous energy protecting their piece of the pie.

Cutting headcount without re-engineering work processes or increasing technological efficiency only piles more work on the survivors. The work doesn't end but there are fewer bodies to execute. After downsizing, 33% of responding companies said they had terminated employees in vital positions. They filled the gap by using temporary workers (43%) or hiring back former employees (35%) or contract workers (28%) in newly created positions. [9]

As organizations juggle human capital, how do you keep the talent you really need? "Is there camaraderie? Is there a career path? Is there integrity that makes people feel secure? If so, they will stay," says executive recruiter, Ellen Martin. To keep the best, make sure they have current, competitive skills in their area of expertise and that they continue to develop as people.

Develop a reputation of growing future leaders and you'll attract the best. Identify bright, ambitious people early in their career so you can develop them in-house. Polish off the rough edges and run interference when they make bone-headed mistakes, even when they embarrass you. Be willing to invest in them by giving them a broad circle of responsibilities to expand their skill sets and advance rather than restricting them to known skill sets.

Lay-off rounds from the early 1990s demonstrated how expensive it is to open the door with an attractive buyout package, usually resulting in the loss of key skills.

The unexpected loss of an important executive results in confusion, stress and apathy among the remaining staff. Your best performers are not waiting passively for the ax to fall – 57% have updated their resumes or pursued some form of career or skill development within the two years prior to downsizing.[10]

Lay-offs are different today than what we grew up watching on the nightly news during the late 1980s. Manufacturers, including the big three auto makers, laid off blue-collar employees in predictable cycles of boom and bust, calling them back to work under an elaborate seniority system. Today, when companies cut white collar workers, they unintentionally cut out corporate know-how.

Head count usually creeps back up as soon as the economy rebounds. With estimates of fully loaded replacement costs for exempt employees ranging up to 120% of annual salary, reactionary lay-offs are an expensive and wasteful churn of talent.

Replacing lost talent is an expense many companies don't measure. The total cost to rehire includes human resources time to re-evaluate the position and how it has evolved with company growth and changes then develop a position description after researching the industry for changes in trends and salary.

In addition to advertising costs and hiring bonuses, recruiting fees can run up to 35% of annual salary, and relocation expenses range between $35,000 to $100,000, if selling the executive's home and temporary housing is required.

Executive recruiter, Fran Chargar adds in the lost productivity costs of executives who use their time to review resumes and interview candidates. Once the new executive is in place, it can take months to acclimate to the new culture and become accepted by peers and staff. "The replacement person, once recruited, is then always open to being recruited again. There is more involved in losing a loyal company person than just money," says Chargar.

Even if the organization is lucky enough to fill the position with an internal candidate, they will pay at least an increase of 5% in base salary for the promotion. If the organization is unlucky or unprepared, the internal person will not be ready for the responsibility or will simply not be the best candidate.

Lay-off lessons learned

"Loyalty down begets loyalty up. We live in a competitive world – one cannot expect loyalty without showing it first."
Stuart Karon

There are three truths to winning the talent wars: Our economy contracts and expands in cycles of boom and bust, our labor pool is shrinking and we will be fighting for loyalty for many years to come. These three truths add up to a deadly combination of diminishing loyalty and dwindling labor.

Unfortunately, an entire generation of people has become hardened after a decade of downsizing. They learn all they can and take their talents and skills to the next company. A recent *Fast Company* study found that only 34% of employees worldwide felt a strong sense of loyalty to their employers.[11]

When the economy improves and the labor market tightens up, people can and will name their price. In 2000, almost 25% of workers surveyed planned on leaving the current employer over the course of the year.[12] Imagine walking into your office tomorrow and finding a quarter of your staff has deserted you!

Today our headlines are filled with statistics and lay-off numbers so staggering they take our breath away. We wince when we read about organizations taking advantage of the slow economy to behave badly; refusing to pay the standard two weeks severance for each week worked. Instead, they claim termination due to poor performance (even when annual reviews are good) leaving the not-so-helpless employees to go to the press to shame their employers into offering severance.

Happily, many companies have readjusted their perspective on loyalty and lay-offs. Prior to downsizing, 42% had tried alternatives such as wage and hiring freezes or job sharing.[13] Although these measures were only slightly successful - saving 1% to 10% of jobs - if your job fell into that 1% to 10%, the statistic becomes personally significant. Other companies have redeployed resources by transferring employees with valuable skill sets that are needed in other areas.

As recently as fall of 2001, companies were still searching for alternatives to lay-offs:

- At a small software company called Illumitek, Inc., six of the highest executives voluntarily took a 5% pay cut to save a mid level manager's position.[14]

- Cisco Systems, Inc. offered laid off workers a third of their salary, benefits and stock-option awards for a year to work at a non-profit group already associated with Cisco.[15]

- Charles Schwab Corp. guaranteed a $7,500 bonus to any laid off employee who got rehired within 18 months.[16]

- Accenture offered as many as 800 consultants 20% of their salaries to take a voluntary sabbatical for 6 to 12 months.[17]

During the talent wars of the late 1990s, these companies faced formidable challenges in recruiting and retaining top talent. Even deep in the throes of recession, they realize the value of rehiring laid off workers.

Today, loyalty is as a revolving door bringing back former employees with needed skills and experience. "When people leave, they are not the enemy; they have not betrayed the company. Rather, they have become alumni. They will return more seasoned and they will stay," says executive recruiter, Martin.

A new look at loyalty

"People today sign on for now versus forever. There is no going through good and bad times. They don't have any illusions that the company will keep them in the next economic downturn."
Cyndy Karon

It may seem old fashioned or hopelessly naive to have any discussion or expectation of loyalty in the aftermath of massive lay-offs. Isn't it more sophisticated to argue we are all free agents, that each of us is responsible for managing our own career? Aren't we supposed to take our toolbox of skills and sell our services to the highest bidder?

However, the clear message from over 100 interviews showed that, although organizations have changed a great deal in the past 10 to 15 years, people have not, human nature has not. People still long for loyalty.

It is not the need for loyalty that has declined, but the application. People today are loyal to their own careers and their profession. Tom Koentop of Lee Hecht Harrison says, "When you leave a company you only leave behind the job title, not the skills and abilities. Loyalty has been reframed as doing a good job while I'm here, but I may not stay. I have to watch my own career, but while I'm with you, I'll give my best."

The problem is that organizations need loyalty more than ever before. In our hyper-competitive business environment where new products proliferate like mushrooms after a hard rain and competitors spring up overnight, organizations desperately need the unconditional cooperation and commitment of their people. How do we meet that need and recapture lost loyalty?

"You must first be loyal to yourself. If you follow someone, he may lead you in the wrong direction," says banker, Eddie Barber. Decide where your first loyalty lies. Are you loyal first to your own career? To your boss? Should your first loyalty be to the organization's objectives? Should you be loyal to the faceless shareholders? It is important to be honest about your first loyalty to give full commitment.

Finding your first loyalty leads to hard questions about larger issue of priorities. Should you be loyal to organizational goals when they conflict with family commitments? Which loyalty takes priority when your boss asks you to travel Monday through Friday? What if you have to take a months-long assignment out of town just to keep your job?

Should you be expected to remain loyal to an organization when the bottom drops out of your stock options?

Should your first loyalty be to your own career when a tempting offer comes along? Can you leave behind the people you hand picked and brought into the company?

Like all difficult questions, there are no easy answers. First loyalty decisions must be grounded in your values. When you operate from a core set of values, first loyalties fall into place. Other loyalties and priorities then stack up like building blocks, allowing you to reach organizational objectives and serve the shareholders.

Individual versus organizational loyalty

One thing that hasn't changed in a decade of downsizing is who goes and who stays. Regardless of why the company is downsizing, the most likely to be laid off are middle management

(43%), clerical and secretarial (28%) and technical (27%) people.[18] Sometimes we get so caught up in the costs of replacing executives we overlook the value of our assistants. They keep us on schedule, tell us who we are eating lunch with, and juggle the million and one details so we can do our jobs.

When I worked for McGraw-Hill in Columbus, Ohio I had the greatest assistant. Cathy didn't exactly work for me, because, if you've ever had a great assistant, you realize that you actually end up working for them. They tend to be very bossy, telling you when to go to meetings and where you're traveling.

We made a great team at McGraw-Hill and accomplished a great deal. But when Home Depot called, I ran off to Atlanta to fast-forward my career. When I got settled, I needed an assistant. I reviewed resumes and interviewed 10 to 12 candidates, all fully qualified. But as I slogged through interview after interview, as competent as the candidates were, they weren't Cathy.

My boss got tired of hearing me complain. Finally he said, "Why don't you stop whining and go get Cathy?" I thought my chances were slim. Back in 1992, Home Depot was a regional company. Back then, no one had even heard of them in Columbus, Ohio.

Cathy had a successful career at McGraw-Hill. She had a good marriage to an architect, who had built her a house on a hill, complete with a full glass front. She had aging parents and a college-age daughter living in Columbus. She had a whole life. I didn't think she would come. But I laid out my best arguments and booked a flight to Columbus. I took Cathy to lunch and we talked and caught up on each other's lives over ribs and onion rings. I kept selling the company in a subtle fashion. As we polished off the last of the onion rings and wiped the grease off our fingers, I gathered up my nerve to ask.

"Um, Cathy, I know you're very happy and successful and have this great life in Columbus," I started, stumbling over the words. "But would you maybe, possibly, think about coming to Atlanta and interviewing with Home Depot?"

I didn't get any farther. Cathy laughed and pulled a ticket to Atlanta out of her purse. She said, "I was just waiting for you to ask!"

Cathy was loyal to me during the good times of building the department and the bad times prior to my divorce. When I left the company, I returned that loyalty by ensuring her position. Today Cathy is very successful at Home Depot, with two assistants of her own. Her continuing contribution to the company lasted much longer than any operational changes I made during my tenure.

Recapturing lost loyalty

"Work is more than a paycheck; it is an opportunity for growth."
Don Schneider, Schneider National

Schneider's company is the largest full-truckload carrier in North America. Its revenues of $3.1 billion in 2001 make it almost twice the size of its closest competitors. Its success comes, in part, from Schneider's belief that people are important. "The role of the organization is to ensure people get more than a good paycheck. We believe in competitive compensation. Work has a large impact on how you think about yourself," says Schneider.

Sometime we forget the real reason why people work. A study by the Human Resource Institute found that over 90% said providing challenging work, paying for increased contributions and offering outstanding training and education opportunities were the top three reasons for staying with an organization.

"Work is a good opportunity to allow associates to grow as human beings by the challenges they face. They can grow in all parts of their lives," says Schneider. He tells the story of a 30-year associate who said, "This company has meant so much to me. My husband left me with three children to raise. In my work, I could see that I was competent and that I could handle the challenges in my family."

Dr. Stephen Taylor of Mississippi State University has done in-depth research on turnover. He found that the most important organizational values for retention are: ethical behavior, valuing honesty and treating people fairly and with respect.

A supporting study by the Ethics Resource Center found that 4 in 5 people say their organization's integrity was an important consideration and 79% said their organization's concern for ethics and doing the right thing is an important reason why they continue to work there.[19] This integrity strengthens the company's shared principles and sense of purpose, bringing out the best in its leaders.

Integrity, values and retention

"If my beliefs and actions are consistent with the organization, they will be loyal to both."
Jim McCallie

A company's reputation for integrity has impact on its ability to recruit and retain employees. A KPMG 2000 organizational integrity study found that 81% of employees who believed their company would not authorize improper conduct would recommend the company. Only 21% of those who believed that management would authorize improper ethical conduct would make a recommendation.[20]

Company values play a critical role in retention, giving people meaning and mission in their work. After I left Home Depot, I joined Dollar General where I worked with people like myself who had grown up poor. We used our education and professional abilities to help low income customers stretch every dollar.

You can create that level of meaning and purpose in your leadership. Communicate the values of the organization by living and breathing them; model them in your everyday behavior.

"It almost seems easy, but it isn't – you must give your people unwavering love," says Jimmy Ardell. It's easy to respect the abilities of your best and brightest – your up-and-coming managers, the ones who thrive on challenge and responsibility. Your dream employees to whom you can hand off a project with full confidence that it will be well executed.

It's harder to offer the same level of respect to Martha, in the back office, who has been with the company 100 years or to hourly employees out on the floor. As a newly minted business graduate from The Ohio State University, I remember how hard it was to live on $7.00 an hour during my starving student days. When one of my fellow graduates called his hourly employees "scum balls," I was too shocked to respond. Then I realized his parents had paid his way through school. He'd never had to live on macaroni and cheese or worry about the light bill. He didn't respect his people and they responded in turn. Even Martha deserves to be respected as a source of company history.

One way to show respect is through the paycheck. At Home Depot we operated under the simple philosophy of, "we pay people what they are worth." This philosophy and the company's reputation attracted the very best candidates, over 100 applicants for each position. Today we face an ever-widening gap between executive compensation and the hourly employees on the front lines. The minimum wage has remained constant at $5.15 per hour for six years. One in 10 families live below the official poverty line of $17,463 for a family of four.

Fight for your people – get them the money and promotions they deserve, especially the old timers whose careers were overlooked or sidetracked a long time ago. Praise and recognition are great motivators but they can't replace fair compensation.

Reward your best performers proportionally – when they perform like stars, pay them like stars.

Face the future with confidence

When times are tough, companies are tempted to squeeze every last nickel out of human resources. Employees operate in a fog of fear that their job could end after one bad quarter. People need some measure of security that their job will last longer than next week.

This short sightedness becomes magnified at the corporate level. People are afraid to take risks beyond this quarter when the company is overly preoccupied with the bottom line and this quarter's results. They have little incentive to invest time and energy in long-term projects when they are uncertain they will be there to see the pay-off.

When they feel their position could end at any time, they will focus on short-term fixes, slapping on a band-aid to stop the bleeding. People can tell the difference between the need for organizational profit and greed. Organizational greed is echoed in individual behavior when people no longer believe they have a future. They maximize money and stock options today because they can't wait around for lengthy vesting schedules or work their way through the ranks.

As a leader, be a source of stability your people can depend on. Be a consistent leader, projecting confidence in the company's future, especially during tough times, to give your people encouragement, focus and direction.

Keep steady under pressure – if you can't fake it, wait to fall apart with trusted friends outside the company. Don't let your people see you ride the roller coaster between euphoria and despair. There is nothing worse than not knowing what to expect when you walk into your bosses office.

Stay the course and have the commitment to see plans through the tough times. Of course you need to be adaptable, but your people need a course of action that doesn't change every year with every new management fad.

Early in my career I sat around a long polished conference table with a dozen of my peers. The executive vice president leading the meeting told us, "Each of you are the leaders of tomorrow – you will take the company to the next level." We all wanted to believe him. We sat up a little straighter, suddenly felt more important, shouldering the new weight of responsibility on our shoulders.

Some days it is difficult to rise above the daily fray and pitched heat of battles, but you must stay focused on the future. Your people need to see your confidence and understand how each of them plays a part in reaching that future. Paint a picture of the organization's long-range goals and strategic direction. Communicate a clear vision of what needs to be done consistently and frequently. About the time you become tired of saying it, they will finally hear and believe it. Energize them toward the overarching goals by tying each employee's performance goals to the vision.

Encourage your people to become visionary leaders; let the vision ripple and cascade through the department. During tough times, people need to commit to great undertakings that will make a great difference. They need a reason for sweat and sacrifice. They need hope.

Without a clear vision, leadership is incomplete; people get lost in ambiguity and the anxiety of fighting fires and they lose heart.

Become bonded

"In judo competition, you are standing very much alone on the mat. You can't seek help – judo people tend to be very self-sufficient. It is an isolating kind of sport. A lot of times, the burden of the sport becomes enormous. You can burn out that way very quickly."
James Bregman, 1964 first Olympic Judo team

It is not unusual to spend more of our waking hours with the people we work with every day than we do with our friends, spouses and children. We form deep friendships that cement the bond of loyalty. A few weeks after I left Dollar General, I got a call from a former colleague. "I used to talk to you two or three times a day, every day," he said. "Now you haven't called in three weeks."

In spite of these bonds, most of us have relocated repeatedly, chasing our career, moving far away from our extended families. The people we work with become our second family, giving us that sense of belonging.

People can be intensely loyal to an organization when they become bonded toward a common goal. So develop an atmosphere that encourages everyone to do well rather than one that pits your people against each other in Darwinian struggle where only the strongest or most Machiavellian survive. Expect your people to do more than simply march in the same direction; expect them to encourage and support each other along the way.

You may not be there forever – you could be downsized tomorrow, take early retirement or receive an offer too tempting to pass up. How will they carry on without you? Just fine if you've laid a foundation of helping one another succeed.

Help your people to act altruistically and to have a generosity of spirit. Show and tell them repeatedly that there is enough for all and that they don't have to be on guard against the opportunism of co-workers or the boss.

Support a full life

"Put your people ahead of Wall Street."
Tim Barber

We all operate within the context of what the company can offer for better work-life balance: flexible hours, compressed workweeks, part-time work and telecommuting. You can encourage your people to maximize the benefits program - to juggle work demands with outside obligations without fear that their boss is questioning their commitment. Don't inadvertently force your people to choose between the conflicting loyalties of family happiness and career advancement.

Sometimes we try to lead as if we operate in a vacuum devoid of the messiness of children, divorce or aging parents. The reality is that we all have lives outside the office that affect how we perform at work. We operate within the framework of a larger social context and a widening disconnect between our sterile office environment and the rest of our lives.

After 9/11, the value of family and friends rose in importance while the traditional values of the organization have lagged far behind. Today, those who've been downsized are less willing to relocate, more willing to take a lesser position to avoid disrupting family life. People who, five years ago, would have moved for a promotion will turn it down if they are not sure their sacrifice will be reciprocated with company loyalty. They will put family stability first.

Letting go

"When you promote up, you suffer a little, but the feeling you get offsets the short term loss."
David Miles

A company sends a message that it doesn't expect people to hang around for long when it doesn't offer training or pay for continuing education. Be honest – is training an expense or an investment in your company? When you draw up budgets, is it the first line item to be cut? Are you investing in your people and their future?

If you make the investment, if you consistently talk up your people like they are the company's greatest assets, they will be pirated away to other functions. Think of it as sowing the seeds for senior management throughout the organization. When the time comes that you have taught them all you can teach, transfer your brightest stars to another department. When they need to round out their experience, be willing to let them go.

Occasionally you'll even need to encourage them to take that tempting offer in another organization. If their careers hit a long plateau or if they make too many mistakes fresh out of college, they could become typecast forever as young and inexperienced. Help them decide if they need to move on to another company to gain respect as a professional. Remember that loyalty can be a revolving door – they will return more seasoned and they will stay.

Loyalty in an individual sport

"Loyalties are a result of mutual trust and benefit. Mutual trust will lead to uncommon acts of courage and it can lead to success. Success, in the sense that you have lived a decent life and you have honored the commitments you set out, and you have been loyal to your principles. That's where the rubber meets the road in judo. Somehow in this sport, you develop a sense of principle."
James Bregman, 1964 first Olympic Judo team

Judo is an individualist sport. The loneliest I have ever been in my life is standing at the edge of the mat, waiting to compete. There is no team, just you and your opponent, putting it on the line. Success is completely dependent upon your performance, your hours of training and techniques, your courage and heart.

Because you are very much alone in competition, judo people tend to become very self-sufficient. Kimberly Ribble, Canadian

Olympian, 2000 Sydney Games, learned some hard lessons about loyalty. Kimberly's loyalty to her first coach cost her a junior competitive career. Her loyalty to her second coach and hometown, won her the admiration of all of Canada.

It took Kimberly 20 years of training and dreaming to become an Olympian. In less than two minutes her Olympic dreams were shattered.

As a child, Kimberly never walked; she ran everywhere. She was a naturally gifted athlete, excelling at every school sport. Growing up, Kimberly felt like an outsider in her family, the only athlete, Kimberly rebelled by not drinking or smoking like the rest of her family. Sports gave her a way not to go home. Kimberly started judo at age seven; judo quickly became her life and preservation. She never had a junior competitive career. Her coach never allowed her to compete nationally; he was afraid another coach would see Kimberly and steal her away.

Kimberly's grandparents scanned the papers, clipping judo articles for Kimberly. They asked her repeatedly to train at Kawasaki's Rendokan Club, winner of regional and national tournaments. But Kimberly was loyal to her first coach.

At 17, Kimberly drove ten minutes across town. Under Coach Kawasaki she started judo all over again. Kimberly had to relearn and correct all of her techniques. It took 10 more years to become an Olympian. Kimberly started from the bottom and fought her way to the top. She kept her sights on the next level, fighting and winning medals, always working towards the next level.

After 20 years of sweat and pain and dedication, the Olympics became the next level.

Kimberly drew the Cuban for her first match in Sydney. The Cuban girl had beaten her in a previous competition with a minor score - Kimberly vowed to give her the best fight of her life. The match started with grip fighting, each girl trying to get a dominant grip on the other's judo gi to throw. When the referee called "Matte" (stop) the Cuban girl lunged at Kimberly's knee. The controversial attack after the referee's "Matte" made the crowd go wild, whistling stomping and shouting as Kimberly writhed in pain.

Kimberly lay on the ground wondering, "Can I stand?" In Olympic Judo, competitors are only allowed one minute for medical evaluation. She told the doctor, "Don't pull me out, I'm going to fight."

Kimberly stood on one leg and continued to fight. The Cuban kicked at Kimberly's injured knee, knocking her down. The Cuban came in for a low throw, dropping to her knees. Kimberly blocked. The Cuban spun around and lunged at her injured knee, catching the heel. Kimberly heard a crack. She thought, "Please let her scream." Kimberly screamed first.

Kimberly went down to the mat and couldn't get back up – she looked at the clock; five seconds left. Her only goal was to finish the match. She begged the doctor, "Let me fight, let me fight." Kimberly went into shock and was rushed to the hospital with broken and displaced bones in her right foot. She spent the rest of the Olympics in a cast.

Kimberly's story went out over the international newswire. She returned to Canada a hero. She spoke in schools and received well wishes from strangers in grocery stores. Today, as Kimberly heals, she puts all her efforts into coaching the next generation of Olympians.

Kimberly has no trace of bitterness over losing her life long dream. She says, "I don't think I'm anybody special. I had a dream. I went and did the best I could and I came home. My loyalties lie here with my city and sensei. Now I'm a role model for little girls, but I am still being me. I was the only one who chose to stay."

Rebuilding trust after lay-offs

In judo, trust is critical. You trust your partner to throw you cleanly and safely. You trust that your opponent will release the arm bar when you surrender before your arm breaks. You trust that the referee will stop the choke if you slip into unconsciousness before tapping out. Because of its physicality, judo is not possible without trust.

Trust is like taking a leap of faith. Over years of practice, there have been many occasions when sensei would instruct the class to do a technique that I was convinced I could not do. After much gathering up of courage, I would try the technique, only to stop short, my mind shouting, "Are you crazy? You'll get killed." I have learned that trust requires taking a deep breath, clearing my mind, and taking that leap of faith, trusting that my body will carry me through.

Trust is at the core of loyalty in leadership. We build trust with our children by taking care of their physical needs as infants, their emotional and intellectual needs through the turbulent teenage years. We provide guidance through the prolonged adolescence of young adulthood.

Painstakingly, we build trust in those we lead through time and through thousands of daily interactions. But trust is a fragile commodity that can be wiped out in one lapse of character, one yielding to the weakness of expediency.

In the early and mid 1990s, we built trust by navigating rope courses and completing weekend team building exercises. Back at the office, if politics and infighting are encouraged and ruining careers is considered sport, all the weekend team and trust building exercises will never be more than shallow diversions.

Too often, in the heat of political battle, we excuse our actions by saying, "It's not personal." Of course it's personal. When company politics affects your livelihood, your ability to pay the mortgage or a child's continuation at a beloved school, it's personal.

Trust and loyalty are built slowly, not in weekend workshops but through leading with honor in good times and bad. Trust is built through years of consistency.

Like all traits of strong character, trust starts from the top, trickling down through the organization. When management acts in an untrustworthy manner, it sends shock waves through the organization. You can't change the character - or behavior for that matter - of top management, but you can act trustworthy and create your own trickle-down effect through your managers, your front line supervisors and your hourly employees.

Downsize with a heavy heart

"The day I feel good about terminating someone is the time to leave."
Gary Salters

When you've nurtured and developed and challenged your team and made them the best there is, that doesn't necessarily protect them from corporate downsizing. A man came up to me after a presentation with tears in his eyes. He had 48 hours to decide which of his people to cut: A man who had been with the company for 25 years and had a wife dying of cancer. A man with three small children and a wife to support. Or himself; but he had a pregnant wife who didn't work.

These are Solomon-like decisions. Lacking Solomon's wisdom, I could not tell him to cut the baby in half. Truthfully, he wasn't asking me to make his difficult decision. "But, if I make this sacrifice, will they remember me?" he asked. "Yes," I told him, "I promise they will."

Sometimes there is no good solution except downsizing. We can choose only the lesser evil, what will hurt the least. Sometimes we get caught up in power struggles and the high stakes of influence and money and forget that people are more than their work identity. They are not interchangeable pieces or title boxes on an organizational chart.

They have families and mortgages - cuts must be made with compassion. Today, people don't expect lifelong employment, but they do expect to be treated fairly and with respect.

We can't always lessen the trauma, but we can soften the delivery of the news. Don't delegate your downsizing to human resources - like nurses; they can act with detachment in the wake of carnage. Don't downsize by memo, fax or voice mail.

Be responsible for your people. As painful and stressful as it is to look someone in the eye and tell them they are losing their job, they are your people. Explain the criteria used to decide who would be downsized and the reasons for the lay-offs. Don't hide behind euphemisms or corporate mumbo-jumbo. Be honest, be direct, and be clear.

Don't do lay-offs in stages, creating an atmosphere of panic. I once worked for a company that undertook massive lay-offs. People refused to answer their phone because they were afraid it might be HR calling them down to collect a pink slip. It is better to rip off the band-aid in one swift movement instead of peeling it back slowly and prolonging the agony.

Communicate from the head and the heart. We often get squeamish when talking about emotions, especially the strong emotions aroused by fear. We would rather keep our emotions safely tamped down - better to bury them in drink, overeating or other self-destructive behaviors.

When a director of human resources advised me to become calloused to terminating people as part of my professional development plan, I knew it was time to leave. She was wrong. I don't ever want to become so hardened that someone losing his or her job doesn't bother me. News of downsizing should be delivered with a heavy heart.

Tell the truth

"Always be honest about bad news – always tell the truth – if the news is bad, tell it fast."
Stuart Karon

And news of downsizing should be delivered honestly. Middle managers often get sandwiched between senior management and the people they lead. They must put a good face on bad news or a flawed strategy, even when fearing for their own jobs. It is especially difficult to manage a workforce when you know a certain percentage won't be there next year. It is difficult to engage people and get their full commitment when they know they may not be there next week, next month, next year. We used to say it was bad luck to take a departmental group photo because invariably we would look at it a year later and count the missing faces.

During the high stress and anxiety of lay-offs, information becomes golden. Trust is built by sharing information, both good and bad. Show your people financial reports, sales forecasts, budgets, anything that helps them understand the company's economic position. You may feel you are protecting your people by not sharing bad news. But in an absence of solid information, rumors will fuel their imagination, painting a far worse picture. Your people often believe you have access to more information than you do. Trust them with what you do know, share everything you can while respecting and protecting confidentiality.

Sometimes we don't want to listen to our people because their bewilderment and anxiety mirrors our own. Sometimes we don't want to hear the truth, feeling powerless to change the company. Other times, all you can do is execute orders and do your best to protect your people. You can't fix it all and you can't have all the answers, but you can really listen. By listening to the complaints and hidden subtext, you can gauge their level of cynicism and commitment. How do they feel about what senior management is doing? If you can't listen without defensive shields going up, use the company's intranet to solicit input and feedback.

After downsizing, there are fewer layers and less checks and balances for behavior. Do you trust the people who work for you? Can you really trust them with power and responsibility? Do you trust their creativity and their drive? Do you trust that they are loyal to your leadership – to the department and company goals? Are they using their talents to better the organization?

As leaders we must entrust our people with power and responsibility. We must trust in their intelligence and drive and that they will perform to the best of their ability. We must believe in their character. This higher level of trust creates greater productivity, morale and loyalty.

Refocus on the future

After lay-offs, there is a period of grieving and reminders of loss: an empty desk, more work and longer hours. Re-focus those you lead by sharing the vision of where the company is going. Let your people know that you are locked into battle together.

Even after downsizing, people are remarkably resilient. They want to believe that management has a plan and that, through their shared sacrifices, the company will emerge leaner, stronger and more competitive. They want to trust that, in the end, they will be part of the pay-off.

Chapter Six

Leadership Questions

- What is the financial impact of lost loyalty?

- Do you prefer that the people you lead be loyal to you or to the organization?

- How do you inspire loyalty in the people you lead?

- How would an organization regain lost loyalty?

Chapter Seven

Living and Leading With Character

Spring 2001

"I said something that shocked me later on. I talked to a reporter after I'd been successful at the Olympic and World Championships, and I said, "You're asking me about fame and all of this good fortune and accolades and it is all very ephemeral. It will all go away, it is not going to last. But what I got out of judo is what is going to sustain me."
James Bregman, 1964 first Olympic Judo team

There are no second chances in competition. There is only split second reaction, full commitment and the roar of the crowd after the big throws.

After I retired from competition, I concentrated on becoming a good referee, finding satisfaction when the right person won the match. But I soon missed the intensity and challenge of competing. As my calendar crept closer to 40, it became dangerous for me to compete against athletes half my age. Yet I was excited to learn the 2001 World Masters Judo Championship, with 450 athletes, was to be held in the United States. I began training in earnest in January.

It took months of daily, dedicated training to reach peak physical condition. I pushed my body hard, one more round of throwing practice, one more punishing grappling round with stronger, faster, heavier partners. I went home alone after practice and ate bran cereal when the team went out for pizza and ice cream. Still three pounds over my competition weight, I woke early and ran, legs heavy as lead.

In practice, I spun out of falls, landing on my shoulder to avoid the score. My body was sure, surer than my mind. My body was ready to win, but my mind needed time to catch up to newfound abilities. I felt the weightless effortlessness of executing a perfect throw; the moment when time stands still, suspended in air, launched through space. Time then, snapping into fast-forward with the thud of landing. I ended practice drenched in sweat, muscles twitching with fatigue, exhausted yet fully alive.

Three weeks before the competition, my shoulder gave out. It started with a tingle, crept down my shoulder blade, progressing to a slow burn. I gave up weight training, knowing my shoulder could bear the weights or the judo but not both. I ran slowly on the treadmill, burning off the last few pounds. I easily made weight at World Masters, my body leaner, sleeker, moving with the sureness and grace of an athlete, the strength and confidence of a fighter.

But there are no second chances in competition. All the days and dedication of training, all of the sweat and sacrifice, all of the nights of visualization before sleep, were over in a few moments. I accepted my silver with disappointment, but no excuses. I stood on the awards stand, the medal hanging heavy against my neck. Flashbulbs popped as people and the press took photos. "Smile!" someone from the crowd called out. I didn't feel like smiling.

On the long plane ride home, I wallowed in my misery. "It's not fair that I trained so hard and sacrificed so much for a silver. What good came of the countless hours on the mat, cross training with weights, running and counting every calorie?" I whined to sensei who was trying to sleep in the seat next to me. All of that effort wasted, I thought, and sank lower in my seat, swallowed up with self-pity.

Sensei asked, "What have you won? Compare yourself to six years ago when you walked into the practice center, overweight and out of shape – today you are strong and fit. How many 40-year-old women would have the courage to fight in a combative, full contact sport? To compete individually in front of hundreds of spectators and leave it all on the mat?" He went back to sleep.

I sat in silence for a long time, staring out the window as the miles passed under the silver wings of the plane. Slowly my self-pity shifted to the realization that winning was not about gold medals, but what had been learned and what had been gained.

Winning was not the techniques or muscle memory or the newfound abilities of an aging athlete. It was no less than a new life, a life filled with Olympians who overlooked my lack of athletic ability and saw the desire to learn, a life complete with judo friendships from around the world, people who loved me no matter if I won or lost. It was a life filled with hundreds of children who had passed through the practice center; some staying a few months, others for years, a few for life.

In the end, winning was not about gold medals, but about an entire new life carved out of the wreckage of my previous life. In the end, maybe all I was looking for in judo was a return to childhood values, taught over carefully balanced saucers of yellow cake with chocolate frosting and delicate china cups of black coffee.

From individual to organizational

"People are looking for bedrock."
Bill Parsons

We began this book by arguing that doing the right thing always comes down to the individual. Now we must draw back up to 40,000 feet to the organizational level.

In these post-Enron days, clear eyed and hard nosed writers from *Fortune, The New York Times* and *Fast Company* are asking the same question – how do we fix the corruption that threatens our financial markets?

As Paul Krugman writes in *The New York Times*, "Now, as each day seems to bring a new business scandal, we can see the theory's fatal flaw; a system that lavishly rewards executives for success tempts those executives, who control much of the information available to outsiders, to fabricate the appearance of success."[1]

A smattering of pre-Enron scandals - Columbia HCA, Waste Management, Rite Aid, Lucent, and Sunbeam - shook investor confidence, yet never made front page news. It took the destruction of shareholder wealth with the Enron collapse ($60,000,000,000) and MCI WorldCom bankruptcy ($175,000,000,000)[2] for corporate corruption to leap from the financial pages to national news.

When we read about billion dollar losses in stock market equity, the numbers seem so large they lose all meaning. It takes an unfathomable nine zeros to make a billion.

But it isn't really the $60 billion lost or $175 billion lost or even the nine zeros. It isn't vague terms like destruction of shareholder wealth that has plunged us into a bitter bear market.

It is one individual investor at a time – the elderly couple who can't afford to retire after their 401(k) was wiped out, the parents who can't afford to send their children to college after 20 years of savings evaporated overnight. It is you and me, the small investors feeling the pinch as our comfortable life cushion shrinks uncomfortably.

During the boom, we deluded ourselves that we were in a New Economy; that the old rules of revenue no longer applied. We crossed our fingers and closed our eyes and rode the wave as stock prices rose to dizzying new heights that ultimately were unsustainable. Now we are nursing a debt hangover from the $9 trillion market drop.[3]

Today, the press bashes CEOs for go-go greed, for their short-term obsession with meeting quarterly profit forecasts and for doing anything to keep the share prices up. But if we are honest, many of us got caught up in the greed-is-good mentality during the late 1990s when it seemed that everyone was getting rich and no one was getting hurt.

Today we've come to realize that accounting fraud is not a victimless crime and that white-collar crooks are indeed criminals.

Consider that seven months after Enron's bankruptcy, the press reported eight separate corporate scandals and accounting shocks; the SEC started 399 enforcement actions and 112 companies restated their financials.[4] A recent poll revealed that 38% of Americans considered big business as the largest threat to our future.[5]

In the spring before a summer filled with scandals, *Fortune* magazine argued, "In this age of the 401(k), when the retirement dreams of middle-class America are tied to the integrity of the stock market, crooks in the corner office are everybody's problem. And the problem will not go away until white-collar thieves face a consequence they're actually scared of - time in jail."[6]

Krugman goes on to state, "Now distrust of corporations threatens our still-tentative economic recovery; it turns out greed is bad after all. But what will reform our system? Perhaps corporations will reform themselves, but so far they show no signs of changing their ways."[7]

Since 2000, we watched fraud unfold from Columbia HCA to Waste Management. Formerly celebrated CEOs, including Chainsaw Al Dunlap at Sunbeam, became villains. With each new scandal, we expressed outrage. We demanded punishment as the unlucky shareholders rode the stock down to the bitter end. Then we lost interest until the next scandal hit the headlines. We simply didn't have the stomach to send our captains of industry to jail. Will this time be any different? It is too soon to tell.

A year ago, we would not have believed that we would witness carefully choreographed perpetrator walks with executives hauled off in handcuffs or that the Big Five accounting firms would be reduced to the Final Four.

Today, sobered by a bitter bear stock market, we are clamoring for honest stock evaluations and business ethics. But what will happen in two years or five years when memory fades? Ten years from now, will we endure another round of slight of hand accounting scandals?

If we are to have lasting change, we must recognize that cooking the books is not the problem plaguing corporate America. It is simply a symptom of a deeper malaise. Corruption has slowly crept into our business culture. Consider these five examples:

- Arthur Andersen verified the accuracy of Enron financials to protect $52 million paid annually in consulting fees, then destroyed documents to stop the SEC investigation. After Andersen was convicted of obstruction of justice, the Big Five became the Final Four. A post script: Andersen was also the auditing firm for MCI WorldCom.[8]

- Merrill Lynch peddled overpriced Internet stocks that its stock analysts called "dogs" to an unsuspecting public. Why? Hyping the stock as a sound investment instead of conducting objective research protected their banking business. Lynch was fined $100 million and ordered to separate its stock-research and investment banking businesses.[9]

- Seventeen days before he was indicted on charges of trying to evade paying taxes on $13 million of art work, former Tyco CEO Dennis Kozlowski told college students, "You will be confronted with questions every day that test your morals. Think carefully and, for your sake, do the right thing, not the easy thing."[10]

- The Big Five, now the Final Four, helped U.S. companies establish corporate headquarters in Bermuda to avoid paying taxes. Their rationale - staying competitive in a global economy. But shouldn't companies who profit from a society support it with taxes? Even after a summer filled with scandals, the Final Four continue to lobby against increased reform and regulation of their industry.[11]

- Founder John Rigas and three sons who held top executive positions and sat on the board of Adelphia, the sixth largest cable company, borrowed $2.3 billion in off-balance-sheet loans, largely to buy company stock. The company was delisted by Nasdaq when Adelphia didn't file its 2001 annual report, then defaulted on $1.4 billion in Adelphia convertible bonds. Bankruptcy and an SEC investigation followed. Five Adelphia executives were arrested, including the 78 year old founder, who was marched off in handcuffs.[12]

These widely admired companies and their leaders played fast and loose with the rules. People who didn't need to cheat did, because they could.

On July 30, 2002, President George W. Bush signed a sweeping business reform bill into law. The Sarbanes-Oxley Act of 2002, commonly known as the Corporate Corruption Reform Bill, provides the most far-reaching business regulation since Franklin Delano Roosevelt's administration in the 1930s. Though the SEC bears responsibility for fleshing out the act and enforcing it, highlights of the business reform law include:

Accounting industry regulation

- An independent accounting oversight board will be established to regulate the accounting industry.

- Accounting companies must separate their consulting work from their auditing divisions.

- Congress can increase SEC funding to hire more auditors and investigators.

White collar crime penalties

- Auditors and executive officers face new penalties including fines and up to 25 years in prison for securities fraud. Destruction of documents needed for federal investigations now carries a maximum imprisonment of 20 years.

- CEOs and CFOs who *knowingly* certify false company financials could face prison terms up to 10 years and fines up to $1 million. CEOs and CFOs who *willfully* certify false company financials could face prison terms up to 20 years and fines up to $5 million.

- Defrauded investors have more time to bring lawsuits against companies.

- Whistle blowers have new federal protection against retaliatory discharge.

Personal accountability

- CEOs and CFOs must personally certify annual and quarterly financial reports.

- Companies cannot grant or arrange personal loans (today totaling tens of millions of dollars) to their executive officers and directors.

- CEOs and CFOs must repay (to the company) certain bonuses and share trading profits if the gains were realized as the result of accounting fraud.

- Executives and company insiders must disclose stock sales and purchases within two days to the SEC. Directors and executive officers cannot buy or sell company stock during 401(k) black out periods.

- Each member of a company's audit committee must be independent. This committee will be held more responsible for the appointment, compensation and oversight of the company's outside auditors.

- Corporate leaders convicted by the SEC cannot serve as officers or directors at another publicly traded company.

- Companies must establish corporate codes of ethics for senior financial officers and promptly disclose any change or waiver of its code of ethics.

Today, many questions remain unanswered. Will the corporate reform bill woo investors back to the stock market? Will the beefed up SEC serve faster indictments and more certain fraud convictions to restore public confidence? Will Wall Street allow CEOs to run their organizations with a long-term focus beyond this quarter?

It is too early to tell. We know there are no quick fixes, no sliver bullets and no instant relief from stock market pain. This time we must do more than demand punishment and passively wait for Congressional regulations to save the day. We must do more than blame crooked CEOs and corrupt accountants. We must pay attention while the current crop of scandals unravels.

Certainly we need enforcement of existing laws and regulations. Clearly we need stiffer penalties - executives who raid corporate coffers should swap their pin stripes for horizontal stripes. But legislation alone will not correct corruption. More rules and harsher penalties won't fix our corporate crisis.

The responsibility for organizational integrity must start with the organization's framework and end with individual accountability. Federal regulations and organizational ethics statements simply act as the white lines on either side of the road; giving us freedom to drive fast within the boundaries.

As all of the much publicized perpetrator walks with executives hauled off in handcuffs has shown, it isn't a faceless organization doing wrong. It is individuals within their organizations making mistakes in a misguided attempt to please their bosses and Wall Street. We cannot legislate our way to organizational integrity.

Integrating individual and organizational

"Integrity keeps you centered with some greater sense beyond your job."
Tom Koentop

In the beginning of this book, I suggested that responsibility to do the right thing belongs to the individual, supported by an organizational framework of ethics. The business ethics movement has been more than 25 years in the making. Today, over 100 colleges have chairmanships in business ethics. More and more colleges are including ethics courses in their business degrees.[13]

Most large companies have met the U.S. Sentencing Commission's Guidelines for Ethics programs. They have published ethics codes and hotlines for reporting misconduct. Thousands more companies have established codes of conduct and require their employees to sign thick codes of ethics written in legalese. Over 800 ethics officers ensure compliance with complex laws and a bewildering blizzard of federal regulations.

We have made progress. But it is not enough. Ethics policies may protect companies from criminal penalties, humiliating headlines and expensive lawsuits, but they are not a panacea. Codes of conduct may prevent illegal conduct but not improper conduct. It is not enough to follow the letter of the law – we must rise above it and lead with honor.

On this issue, renowned economist, Milton Friedmann has been misquoted for almost four decades. In 1964, his assertion that management is "to make as much money as possible..." was widely quoted. However, most dropped the rest of his quote, which was, "...while conforming to the basic rules of society, both those embodied in the law and those embodied in ethical customs."[14]

No one questions that profits are the lifeblood of an organization. But somewhere along the way, we lost sight of the reality that organizations have responsibilities beyond making their quarterly numbers and meeting Wall Street expectations. Today, top business publications remind us of those responsibilities.

Fast Company writes, "We used to recognize corporations as both economic and social institutions – as organizations that were designed to serve a balanced set of stakeholders, not just the narrow economic interest of the shareholders."[15]

What then are the responsibilities of organizations? Should they be expected to do more than the bare minimum of sticking to the letter of the law? Is it enough not to cook the books, cheat suppliers or foist overpriced and unsafe products on an unsuspecting public with caveat emptor?

If we are to change American business, we must realize afresh that we serve more than Wall Street; we serve the shareholders, our employees, our communities and the environment. We can't be forced to choose between integrity or profits; rather we must strengthen the relationship between financial performance and social responsibility.

In 1970, Pax World, the first socially responsible mutual fund, promised no stocks in defense, nuclear power, gambling, alcohol or tobacco. Pax World sought out environmentally friendly stocks in companies who hired women and minorities.[16] Following that lead, social investors today control more than 12 percent of the managed assets in the United States.[17]

As fund managers search for socially responsible stocks, they are adding a fifth stakeholder, still undefined, still un-quantified, but it is certain that white-hat stocks must include ethics, writes Jane Bryant Quinn.[18]

A summer of corporate scandals has raised questions not heard since the hand wringing of the Reagan administration's welfare reform.

Today, there is a gaping economic divide between CEOs and front line workers – the people who pull orders, ring up purchases, the customer service voice on the other end of the phone. After years of shrugging off reports of outrageous executive compensation packages, we've found fresh outrage.

During the 1990s, "...(executive compensation) rose by 570%. Profits rose by 114%. Average worker pay rose 37%, barely ahead of inflation, which went up by 32%. In 1999, while median shareholders' return fell by 3.9%, CEO direct compensation rose another 10.8%," reports *Fast Company*.[19]

"If everyone's compensation had risen as fast as CEO's during the 1990s, the average production worker would now earn nearly $125,500 and the minimum wage would stand at $25.50," writes Quinn.[20]

Should we allow the free market to set the minimum wage? Should business be concerned about narrowing the widening rift between the haves and have-nots? How do we help those who never seem to get past the first rung of the economic ladder? Is our responsibility to stop the slide toward a society of the immensely wealthy and desperately poor? We've always known that the rich get richer while the poor get poorer, but now we understand that wide compensation gaps can lead to misconduct.

We have grown weary and wary of the worn out clichés of lean and mean companies. "Enron, Andersen, Global Crossing - these business catastrophes are merely the tip of a black iceberg. Under the surface lies a culture that is increasingly defined by selfishness. Consequently, the public's confidence in business and large-scale institutions has been shaken," reports *Fast Company.*[21]

In the end, doing what is right always does come back to the individual. It begins with the most basic leadership skills, supported by the organizational framework. It ends with no less than creating a new corporate culture. "Of all the factors that lead to corporate crime, none comes close in importance to the role top management plays in tolerating, even shaping a culture that allows for it. With each wink, nod and nudge-nudge, instructions of a sort are passed down the management chain," writes *Fortune.*[22]

The answer to how can we fix this problem of corruption that threatens our financial markets is not what, but who. The answer is you and me. We can create a company culture where it matters to take a measure of a leader's character.

You can create the kind of company you are proud to lead - not by rigidly following the rules or by handing down moral authority from on high, like a homegrown version of the ten commandments. Not by dictating your values or trying to force your faith on others.

You do it by helping the people you lead understand their values and by helping incorporate their core values into the organization's values. You do it by having your people understand that character is more than following rules and regulations; it is the responsibility of each person. You can communicate your values and the fundamental principles that the company stands for through stories of leaders doing the right thing. You can set the example by living and leading with character.

Character is not a fad or buzzword – rather, it helps you draw on reservoirs of strength when fighting apathy and resistance. It is as simple as it is difficult. Character comes from deep within – it is who you are and what you believe, what you stand for. It takes patience, determination and practice. Character is for those who are tired of the trivial and who have become impatient with quick fixes and empty promises. It is for people who want to live and lead by their strong sense of values in all aspects of their lives.

Character is looking beyond the quick fix and immediate gratification. It takes a measure of unselfishness, a kindness of heart and generosity of spirit. It is having a vision for your life, and the thousand daily acts and decisions that feed that vision. It is the little things that add up to a life well lived. Character is not easy – you will have setbacks and discouragements. It is not always rewarded - sometimes people risk and lose their jobs fighting for what is right.

Inez (a pseudonym) says, "You have to make a decision and stand up for what you believe." Inez learned that she and several other women in the department were paid far less than men with comparable positions were paid. She brought it to management's attention and asked them to correct the inequity. Inez refused an offer of equal pay just for herself. "I wanted to include all who have been done wrong," she says. Her assistant told her, "They'll crucify you for this." Inez stood up for what she believed through ugly repercussion and being pegged as a troublemaker. She said, "My stand was unpopular but it was in the best interests of the company. I damaged my position and ruined any possibility for advancement, but I got raises for the women who were grossly underpaid. It was not right – it was ethically and morally wrong. I could not fight just for myself. I would do it again."

The essentials of character

"When the company folded, the banks were willing to work with me because of the integrity I brought to the table. That integrity mattered more during bad times - those down times - than in good times. Without it, the bank would not have stood behind me."
Mike Mooney

When Ken Fitzpatrick made the transition from a corporate career to entrepreneur, his reputation for integrity was critical to small business success. "At my previous company, I lived by my word. I made $1 million deals based on a handshake and followed through even when it was costly. Today, it is a rarity when a man's word is his bond," he says. "The people in the vendor community were helpful when starting my business. I could not have started without their support. The executive VP of a major supplier calls on Wal-Mart, K-mart, Target and my one store, Card Mart."

Protect your reputation

"In rural America you have to be accountable – you see your neighbor at the ball games and grocery stores."
Eddie Barber

Don't fool yourself that we live in a big anonymous world. What is your reputation worth?

In 1995, I moved from working in Atlanta, a city in those pre-Olympic times of three million, to working in Scottsville, Kentucky, a town of 4,000. It took months to slow my internal pace, to quiet the busyness of my mind. It took a conscious relaxation to step into the slower rhythms of small town living, a place where people know your family and reputation, a place where people don't bother to lock their cars and leave their keys in the ashtray. A community where people are still shocked by bad behavior.

For seven years, I've lived in a small town, growing used to everyone knowing everyone else. But even those who work in large cities live in small neighborhoods. And each of us works in a tightly inter-connected industry within our professional field.

Like most professions, the logistics community has very small circles. During my logistics career, I called my friend Dick Hitchcock before I hired a candidate. Dick knew everyone, at least by reputation. He knew all the skeletons in the closets and where the bodies were buried. He knew if a candidate was honest, competent and respected.

The one time I was in a hurry and didn't call Dick, it was a disaster. The recruiter references came back clean, but the new hire was politically vicious. He used his influence to intimidate vendors into giving him cash gifts and deep discounts on new cars. When he was finally found out and fired, his previous manager called to ask, "What took you so long?"

A worried Sherron Watkins wrote in her memo to Enron CEO Kenneth Lay, "My eight years of Enron history will be worth nothing on my resume." Watkins emerged unscathed, but fellow Enron employees were painted with the broad brush of scandal.

Like a shadow, your reputation is with you every day. It follows you from company to company. It can open or close doors. It can cost you promotions or win you career-building assignments. A good reputation allows you to take risks and promote programs without suspicion of a hidden agenda. It attracts people who want to work for a leader of high integrity.

Being a leader of character means sharing your mistakes and struggles, the times you have fallen short and the lessons you have learned. It is not holding you above the fray with a holier-than-thou attitude - a surefire recipe for disaster.

Larry Mercer of The Home Depot says, "One of the things I had to learn was that the mistakes we make are opportunities to learn. As a perfectionist, when you miss perfection, you quickly spiral down. Mistakes do happen. Every big mistake I've made has come out on the other side better. It is a cliché to say the journey is better than the destination but, as we have more history in our lives, we realize it's true."

Create a common language

"Living an honorable life means we must learn a common language."
Jon Ridley

In the mid 1990s, companies invested significant time and effort developing their mission statements, values and overarching goals. Today, many of these carefully thought out mission statements hang on the wall like a limp rag or gather dust in a drawer. They have become mere rhetoric because they are not reflected in the reality of everyday life.

Teach your people to speak a common language driven by their values. Even if your mission statement was crafted by a gaggle of consultants, you can turn it into a meaningful message by rewriting it in your own words and modeling it for those you lead. Don't merely mouth the words, live and breathe the mission.

Ann Drake, President of DSC says, "I work hard at building mission, vision, values and promise and what it means to my people. In our changing world, it is something they can hang onto – something permanent. We spend so much time at work, they must feel like this is seriously good work."

Teach the next generation

"If you don't have integrity, someone will lead you astray. When the company fired me, they replaced me with a young man who made a lower salary - I had trained him for a year. When I was fired, he didn't even look up from his desk. He later stole $60,000 from the company. That young man didn't get the training he needed in his home life."
George Harris, 1964 Olympian

My first boss at The Limited was a brilliant man; just a dissertation shy of a PhD in mathematics. Whenever we struggled with a difficult decision, he asked two simple questions, "Is it illegal, immoral or fattening?" and, "How would you feel if your decision showed up on the front page of *The Columbus Dispatch* in the morning?"

Throughout my logistics career, I've often repeated those questions to my own young managers. It is important to guide new leaders in the right direction because they will influence many people over a 40-year career. Without your encouragement, it can be difficult to do the right thing when so many decisions today are painted in shades of gray.

The year was 1962. Mary Jo had graduated as valedictorian of her class. She was 18, Larry Netherton was 20. It was a magical time, when everything seemed possible. Mary Jo's father didn't want them to marry. He was afraid they would start a family and never finish college. But love couldn't wait. Larry and Mary Jo ran off and got married against her father's wishes.

Larry says, "We were as independent as hogs on ice." Every Sunday they would eat dinner with Mary Jo's family, but her father refused to speak to them, eating the meal in stony silence. They both started college, but money was tight. Back then; job opportunities for women in Kentucky were scarce. So when Larry was offered a job at the feed mill, he jumped at the chance.

Larry's new boss was an old family friend. He had taken Larry to his first major league ball game. Larry was grateful for the job and gave it his all. He worked hard, starting out with the dirty jobs, unloading boxcars of barbed wire, loading bags of fertilizer on trucks. Larry was smart and eager and soon he was involved in every phase of the operation. He was promoted to typing invoices in the front office.

The office work was clean and easy. But Larry had grown up on a farm. He didn't like to be idle and didn't mind getting his hands dirty. So when the front office was empty he would go back to the dock and load trucks. One day he was working on the dock when his boss told him to get back to the office to waiting customers. He was gruff, telling Larry they were busy. But when Larry went to the office it was empty. After this happened several times, Larry snuck back to the loading dock and hid behind a stack of fertilizer.

Larry discovered his boss was cheating the farmers. He kept the farmer's corn, diluting the dairy cattle's high-analysis feed with inexpensive fillers. He stacked expensive bags of fertilizer on top to hide less grade fertilizer on the bottom. After hours the boss loaded up the corn and the rich fertilizer to take home to his own farm. Larry started keeping track – checking the customer invoice against what was loaded on the truck. The bosses' wife kept the books, so she made sure everything balanced.

Larry learned that baby calves loaned out to poor families on feeding contracts were being taken away before they went to market. Months passed. The cheated farmers' dairy cattle weren't producing much milk. Their crops failed. Poor families lost what little they had.

Larry was racked with guilt and anxiety. What should he do? He liked the man, but hated what he was doing to the farmers. But his boss was a family friend. And he had been good to Larry.

"I couldn't go to my father. What if he knew? Worse yet, what if he were involved?" Larry says, "That was the hardest burden to bear."

Larry went to an older man who had been with the company for 30 years, a man he respected and admired. He shared his suspicions and asked for advice. But the older man was afraid for his paycheck and his pension. He told Larry, "Don't get involved, look the other way."

On November 22, 1963 John F. Kennedy was shot. Larry was in shock. He had traveled to Bowling Green, Kentucky and stood on the sidewalk to watch JFK go by in a motorcade. He thought about how JFK had challenged young people to service. Larry, along with the rest of the country, grieved.

Then he took action. He persuaded the drivers to write down exactly what was loaded on the trucks and compared it to the invoices. They didn't have copiers back then, so Larry made copies on the thermal machine, which was located right next to the desk of the bosses' wife.

Larry turned the documents, all the proof of fraud over to the district manager. The boss and his wife left quietly. No charges were ever filed. The Board of Directors protested their resignation – they could not believe they had been fooled. Larry never told his father.

After six months of silence, his father-in-law began talking as if nothing had ever happened. Larry and Mary Jo went on to earn masters degrees and enjoy successful professional careers. They raised a beautiful daughter and have been happily married for 38 years.

Two questions - what would you have done if you had been in Larry's shoes?

What would you have done if you were the older man, afraid for your paycheck and pension?

Surround yourself with men and women of character

"As your peer group changes, your life changes – surround yourself with people of honor."
Ken Fitzpatrick

Who do you have to encourage and support you? How do you find the strength to do the right thing in the things that don't seem to matter or that no one will ever find out about?

Who acts as your sounding board to call when you're not sure of the correct course of action? We are all subject to peer pressure no matter if we are 14 or 44. If we rely on our feelings or follow laws or social norms, we can drift far from character.

Many of us don't have positive reinforcement. In fact, most people are doing their best with no encouragement or reinforcement. Surround yourself with men and women of honor. It doesn't matter if you find them at your church, Kiwanis or Rotary Club, but surround yourself with people who share your commitment to character. If you can't find an existing group, start your own.

Find a company with core values that compliment what you already practice. Life is too short and careers are too stressful to fight an uphill integrity battle within your organization. Sam Starks gave up a corporate career that compromised his integrity. Today he passes down leadership lessons as he teaches college students. He says, "Working for someone without values will kill your spirit. It was a difficult decision to leave, but I didn't like the company direction. I had to quit to keep Sam being Sam."

Maintain consistency

"Never give up. Just keep trying, keep doing the best you can on a daily basis. Win, lose or draw, get up the next morning, keep trying again. Life is a journey. We don't know where it is going to go, we don't know when it it's going to end, but you have to do the best you can going down the road. The reality is there are good days and bad days, there are heroic days and really dog-eat-dog days. You must maintain a sense of optimism and equilibrium."
James Bregman, 1964 first Olympic Judo team

Throughout my athletic career, I have trained with and competed against athletes with far greater athletic gifts. They stalled out at the green or brown belt level while I went on to earn my black belt. The difference came from consistency in training, competing and developing other athletes.

Living a character-centered life comes from that same dedication to practice and commitment. Character comes from consistency in how we apply the standards we have decided to live by.

It is of no use to be consistent with our moral principles and values if we follow misplaced priorities and values. Character goes beyond competency and managerial skills. It takes courage and heart. But you can't fake it. You can't be a person of character 90% of the time and yield to expediency the other 10%.

Character in all parts of your life

"If you practice integrity in all parts of your life, it is easier to integrate. My honor and reputation should transcend the company."
Fred Ball

All of us face complex issues everyday - at the office, in our children's sports and in our community involvement. Our integrity is tested when we must make split second decisions, like the man who had to decide which three of ten people in his department to cut while his vice president waited on hold. These moments of truth must be grounded in the bedrock of your beliefs.

Challenging his boss cost Bernie Hale promotions, but that wasn't the most important thing. "Your leader may look upon you as if you are being disloyal," says the consultant. "He may want you to follow him whether he is right or wrong. But I made sure my people knew where I stood and it had a ripple effect in the company."

A character-centered life is composed of moments. It comes from doing the right thing and the next right thing and the next, until character becomes a habit and a way of life as natural as breathing.

In 1996, Canadian Olympian Patrick Roberge's final qualification to make the Olympic team for the Centennial Atlanta Games came down to a fight-off. The winner of two out of three matches would win the Olympic spot.

Patrick lost the first match on the referee's decision. In the second match he got his opponent in an armlock. "I did not want to break his arm and end his Olympic dream," Patrick said, "So I applied the armlock very slowly, giving him time to tap out."

Patrick's opponent did not want to surrender so close to making the Olympic team. Patrick continued to crank the arm back slowly giving his opponent no choice but to surrender. Patrick lost the third match on a referee decision.

Afterward, his friends told him he should have broken the arm. But Patrick says, "I felt good because I did it in the way I was taught, to go slowly and give him the choice to surrender or break his arm. I could have gone quickly and that would have meant a spot for me on the Olympic team. I thought about this while I applied the armlock. In competition, you have mere seconds to make those decisions. I decided I would respect the rules and what I had been taught. That match was the biggest challenge to my integrity."

Deciding to live with character may be something you have quietly considered for some time. Character is more than good intentions. It takes practice and unsung successes. It takes small steps toward a new life and regularly scheduled quiet time for reflection.

Living a character-centered life won't happen abruptly. Radical, ill-considered change causes turmoil. Too many losses of familiar landmarks leave us disoriented and discouraged. Like a New Year's resolution to lose weight or stop smoking, such decisions often are quickly abandoned.

Character is not easy. Growth can be painful and uneven. You will make mistakes. Despite the best of intentions, you will backslide into bad habits. You will fall short of the high expectations you set. Choose an accountability partner to encourage you through the setbacks and to push you when you lag behind.

Living with character means having the maturity to accept that there will be temporary setbacks. Sometimes we have to operate within a system that is unethical, unprofessional and unfair. Character is not a panacea for a trouble free life. But it is worth it. Two years of research and over 100 in-depth interviews showed that living and leading with character yields long-lasting, deeply satisfying success.

Chapter Seven

Leadership Questions

- Can you give an example of when you made a difficult but honorable decision?

- How has being a person of character helped you in your career?

- Has there ever been a time when doing the right thing hurt your career?

- How does one lead a character-centered life?

Chapter Eight

Winning Your Way

Summer 2001

By summer of my new business' first year, I was worn out from the 16-hour workdays and worried about whether or not the business would succeed. The learning curve was too steep, mistakes too costly, the clock rapidly running out.

I flew to Dallas to spend two days with a small business consultant. As I voiced my concerns, she asked, "What price are you willing to pay for success?"

I paused, considering the risks and rewards. My business, like a new baby, demands attention. It greedily consumes all available hours. It interrupts sleep. The late nights of work and early mornings of writing leave me as bleary eyed as a newborn's mother.

I thought about the purpose of the business, driven by the message of living and leading with character. I thought of the people I'd spoken to and their hunger for meaning. Their quotes and stories ran through my mind like music.

I paused, considering. I thought about my daughter, nearly grown now; successful and secure, but still needing me. I thought about the fragility of health we all take for granted until it is gone.

I paused, considering where I had been and how far I had come. The path was clear. This time, I will set limits. I will not allow the business to consume my entire existence. I will not return to a life without love, to success without someone to share it. I will not let my daughter become a stranger.

Earlier, in another career, in another life, I had paid a hefty price for success. The cost was too high. "I will not," I decided. "This time, I will not."

A second chance

Sometimes we get a second chance. In 1986 I attended my first Council of Logistics Management Conference. I wore my best (and only) navy blue suit and perched on a chair outside the Women in Logistics reception, counting participants. There were 34 attendees that year. I remember the number because I swiped the "Women in Logistics" poster. I kept it as a promise – a promise of career success for me, and of a better life for my daughter. The poster followed me through my logistics career of a dozen years. It followed me through too many relocations, through marriage and divorce, through career setbacks and successes. It sits silent in the back of my closet, the promise fulfilled

In the fall of 2001, I attended the same logistics conference. At the Women in Logistics reception I looked at my long-time friends in amazement. Overnight, we had become the old-timers.

One of those old friends, Ann Drake, is President of DSC. "When your company reaches $10 million in sales, you can join our 200 club of women presidents," she offered. At this point, my company had not one penny in revenue. I wasn't sure if the business would make it and wasn't counting on an invitation to the 200 club. But I thanked Ann for her belief in me.

Later, I attended a session called "Navigating Midlife Transitions" presented by Jim Warner. The room was packed with young/old people like me.

Jim asked each of us to list the ten most important things in our life. He then asked us to cross them off one by one. He posed this question, "Are you living your life in a way that reflects what is most important to you?" For the first time in my life, I could honestly answer, "Yes." For the first time in five years, I didn't feel caught in crises. I no longer felt like my life was slipping through my fingers like water. I wasn't waking at 3 a.m. worried that I was wasting my life on something that didn't matter. For the first time, in a long time, I was working fully from my strengths. At 40, I was just now hitting my stride, operating at peak performance. I had the peace that comes with answering the call.

Have you taken the time for introspection to imagine your life 10 or 20 years down the road, if you continue on the same path? Picture your life one year before an ideal retirement. You enjoy good health and high energy from taking care of your body. You look forward to life after retirement, to spending more time on your outside interests. Now that you and your spouse are empty nesters, you have a deeper level of love, more time and money to enjoy each other's company. At work, you are widely respected and sought out for advice and mentoring. You have strong relationships with your adult children and the time to enjoy your grandchildren.

This can be your life. You can look back at the end of your career without bitterness or regret. You have a second chance. It starts today.

Finding wisdom

"Everything, every person has something to teach me. Everyone has something you can learn —everything applies – it is how we apply it to our environment."
Karen Galena

This is not a book about what great companies do. Our business libraries are filled with corporate case studies. This is a book about real people, struggling to make sense of our imperfect business environment and hold fast to their values. They have faced temptation - sometimes they have taken the easy way out.

They've been disappointed and discouraged. They are flawed; often they have made mistakes and fallen short.

These real people have shared their hard-won wisdom, their mistakes and their successes with you. How will you put the principles of courage, honor and benevolence into practice in your life?

Like the people in this book, people are put in your path every day to teach you. Their wisdom is all around you, found in the ordinariness of daily life. But you have to listen for it. Wisdom often comes from unexpected sources, at inconvenient times, when we are too tired, too stressed or too hurried to listen.

We have to slow down long enough to listen for it. We must be watchful.

"In the long run you have to live with yourself and what you have done with your life," says Talley Jones. Can we, the baby boomers, maximize this opportunity? What lessons can we learn from 9/11? More importantly, what lessons can we apply?

What can we learn, the generation of whiners who insist someone has to pay every time something bad happens. What can we learn, the generation who wouldn't recognize stoicism if it came up and bit us on the ankle.

What can we learn, the generation that refuses to act like grown ups, the generation that still says, "I don't know what I want to be when I grow up," without irony or embarrassment. What can we learn, the generation that refuses to grow older, holding on to eroding youthfulness by any means necessary - cosmetic surgery, expensive sports cars and even more costly second wives. With work, we can mature into our new roles and become true leaders. We can live our legacy.

As we baby boomers reach our 40s and 50s, we catch a glimpse of our own mortality – the people we grew up with, went to high school with suddenly drop dead with heart attacks or lose their fight with cancer. By the time we reach midlife, we no longer feel invulnerable. We have been sobered, even scared. We have been knocked down; we have faced death and serious illness; we have failed in our marriages and careers. It will take time to heal. But as sensei told me long ago, there is a difference between pain and injury. You must never surrender.

We can live our legacy through mentoring Gen X and Gen Y and passing on our professional and life lessons. Through informal and formal mentoring programs, we can teach positive political skills - how to use relationships and resources for the good of the organization. We can model a solid work ethic, regular attendance, good judgment and old-fashioned values that stabilize an organization.

My journey that has brought me to the end of this book began with one burning question: is it possible for ordinary men and women to lead with character? The answer, after three years of research and interviews is clearly yes. Chapter one asked, "Can ethics be taught?" The answer may be no, but we can support and reinforce the values that are already there. We can give tomorrow's leaders clear direction. We can support them to do what is difficult and right.

People who need us are put into our path everyday. Often we are too busy, too overwhelmed to recognize they are indirectly asking for help. You can make a difference in one person's life and see it flow outward to the many people they will impact throughout their careers. You can help the people around you to be better than they are.

Living your legacy

"The world is changing faster and faster everyday. More and more people are concerned that they will pass without making a lasting impression on the world. They would like to have a part in something that will be a part of the future, to make a meaningful contribution to society."
Ron Tripp, President, USA Judo

Rabbi Kushner writes, "The people who had the most trouble with death were those who felt that they had never done anything worthwhile in their lives, and if God would only give them anther two or three years, maybe they would finally get it right. It was not death that frightened them, it was insignificance - the fear that they would die and leave no mark on the world."[1]

Rather than fantasizing about the legacy left at your funeral, wouldn't it be better to start today, to work toward a living legacy; one where you can see the fruits of your labors?

Last year, Parnell Legros won NYC's Sloan Public Service award from Mayor Rudolph Giuliani. At the award presentation, a reporter questioned his accomplishment - the report that 100% of the poor, mostly black players from the Starrett City public housing project went on to college. Legros' colleagues confirmed the college success rate.

Nine years ago, when Legros started the Starrett Judo Club, he promised the kids if they would give him their full attention and train hard, they could become Olympians. Today, Legros has produced several top-ranked players in the United States, three who are well on their way to making the Olympic team.

Over 1,500 students have passed through the community-based program since 1993. Legros teaches physical education during the day, then coaches an after school judo program at the elementary school five days a week.

Legros feels he is teaching more than judo. He is teaching the kids how to carry on in everyday life. He ends each class with a lecture on the five virtues of respect, humility, generosity, kindness and simplicity. He says, "Without judo, many children could not become a champion. Through judo, we show them a different world – a better world. We give them a sense of hope."

Like Parnell, there are thousands of volunteer, unsung coaches from other sports who have taught children the valuable lessons of sports. They are living their legacy.

Your legacy at home

"My parents were of German-English upbringing. They never said I love you. They died without saying it. Every time my kids take out the garbage I tell them, "I love you."
Tom Koentop

Most of us are not remembered past two generations. We are immortalized only in our genes. Before you dash off to answer the legacy siren song, be sure to take care of your own first. How you live your life most directly affects your children and their children.

"My daughter sent me an email saying, my mom is the greatest mentor," says Executive VP Maria McIntyre. In her 25-year career with The Council of Logistics Management, Maria has been responsible for the education and career advancement of thousands of professionals, yet she proudly references her most important legacy, her daughter.

Of the millions who play amateur sports, only the smallest fractions of them become Olympians. Even the best athletes' competitive careers are short. Many Olympians leave their sport after the spotlight fades. Only a dedicated few develop the next generation of athletes.

Irwin Cohen, the Olympic coach who urged me to retire from competition, is fighting a terminal illness. He fights to fulfill his dream to coach his two sons, RJ and Aaron, at the 2004 Olympic games in Athens.

In Irwin's post-Olympic career, he has produced seven Olympians and one Olympic medalist. He has coached hundreds of children, giving them the self-confidence and work ethic to compete in sports and life.

In the summer of 2000, Irwin had just learned of his illness. He looked tired. Coaching from the mat side, he was quieter, more philosophical with the losses. I didn't see Irwin again for many months. I looked for him during the fall tournament season. His sons were vaguely reassuring.

The following spring, Irwin was far too thin and pale. I didn't recognize him at first. I waited until the shock and fear had faded from my eyes before hugging him hello. Irwin was quiet at the competitions, wrapped tightly in a parka trying to keep warm. He wandered like a ghost, watching his boys who fight every moment of a match and don't know how to quit.

On the last night of Senior Nationals, Irwin sat alone, away from the crowd snapping pictures of the medallists. The boys stood protectively nearby. I stopped in front of him and took his hand. "Will you lend your name to an award for best fighting spirit at Junior Olympics?" I asked. He agreed and joked, "Just don't make it posthumously." I promised and walked into the muggy Orlando night air, sobered.

That summer Irwin looked stronger and tanner, but old laugh lines cut deep grooves beside his eyes. I asked questions about his training and Olympic experience, trying to get the right quote to accompany the Junior Olympic award. But he tired easily. Many questions were left unasked; the right quote proved elusive.

At the end of the tournament, we hugged everyone goodbye and bid them a safe journey home. As sensei and I walked back to our hotel in silence, I remembered a piece of advice Irwin gave me long before he knew he was sick: "Practicing courage in the small acts prepares you for the time you must face down your fear." As we cut across the lawn to the hotel lobby, the wet grass brushed cold against my sandaled feet. I held sensei's hand tightly, shivering in the crisp night air. "We are lucky, aren't we?" I said suddenly, apropos of nothing. "Yes," he agreed, "Yes, we are lucky."

We don't know what life holds. There are no guarantees of longevity or good health, happiness or financial security. But we are lucky. We have a second chance.

Live with courage

"Judo has allowed me to go through almost every minute of my life unafraid, which is a statement that I think, unfortunately, very few women can honestly make."
Ann Maria Rousey, 1984 World Champion

Almost a year after 9/11, we have become accustomed to vague warnings. We brace ourselves for the next attack. We wonder how many will have to die? But we refuse to live in fear. There is a freedom that comes with letting go of fear.

One of my heroes is George Harris, six-time Air Force judo champion, a member of our first judo Olympic team in 1964. Today, George is in failing health. In the past year he has suffered a heart attack, a stroke, and is fighting prostate cancer. But he told me everything that happens to you shapes your values and whether you'll become an honorable person. Lying in his hospital bed, George made his peace. He said, "I am not afraid to meet my Maker." When you live an honorable life, there is no fear in death. Nor in living your life.

In our modern world, we don't get many opportunities to test our courage. Instead, we watch action adventure movies and revel as our on-screen hero overcomes tremendous odds. Few of us have the chance to physically pit our strength, skill and courage against another or make heroic rescues. We never have to face down our fear.

What are you afraid of? Business failure? Bankruptcy? Ask yourself what is the worst that can happen? Lay out the worst case scenario and plan how you would recover. Then release the fear. Let go of whatever is holding you back. Take that leap. Realize that there will never be a convenient time. If you wait for the right conditions, for the right moment, you will never have the courage to begin.

Courage is not the absence of fear, but stepping forward in the face of fear. Practicing courage in the small moments and every day acts will carry over to all parts of your life.

Live in this moment

Live in this moment. When you are at work, work. When you are at home with family, really be with them, don't just pretend. Don't just be physically there while allowing your mind to drift back to the office. Live now, in this moment, in its intensity or even its ordinariness.

When my daughter was young, I used to press down on her head and tease her about freezing her in this perfect age (clearly, this was before she became a teenager).

So often we daydream about the future – how perfect our lives will be when we reach the next big goal: finish school, find the perfect job, get married or reach the next level of financial security. We will be happy when our children are born, or when they finally are out of the house and off to college.

For years I daydreamed about writing this book. I envisioned quiet hours spent sipping coffee and writing in an elegant journal; an oasis of tranquility, working at a languid pace where the words flowed like water. The reality was far different. I labored under self-imposed, impossible deadlines, working 15-hour days and gulping, rather than sipping, coffee by the gallon.

I grew snappish with phone calls and interruptions to my writing. I was distracted, worrying about completing the next chapter. As I labored over each section, writing became a chore, and it showed. The words lay flat on the page like a dead animal.

I took a break for a few days and woke up the next Sunday morning refreshed. I sat and wrote at my kitchen table, the silence broken only by the sounds of birds squabbling over bird seed. I sipped my coffee slowly, the words flowed like water from my relaxed mind and the entire book clicked and fell into place.

Too often we race through our days and weeks, realizing later that we freeze framed the best moments, reliving them in memory instead of living fully in the moment.

Define success on your terms

"If you are not working toward your own goals, you are working toward helping someone else get what they want in life. Don't get trapped following in someone else's footsteps."
Ken Fitzpatrick

The mothers of my judo students are mildly astonished at my lack of domestic skills. Finally one of them spoke up in my defense, "Maybe you can't cook - but you can sure play some kick-butt judo!" she said. That simple comment put it all in perspective. We do best that which we value; we invest time and energy and we get better at it.

Success on your terms sometimes means taking yourself out of the race. Sometimes it means deciding you no longer want to play the game. It is maturity that measures success on your terms, far beyond the fraternity mentality of comparing the size of your house or stock portfolio with that of your neighbor.

Build your Camelot

"In any athletic activity, it's the discipline and loyalty and the principles of the activity that transfer to business life. The corporate culture needs to be nurtured to foster a certain set of guiding principles. If your company doesn't have that corporate culture, a very high level of integrity and a high level of performance, it falls apart. The hardest thing to do is to sustain these efforts over a protracted period of time. Camelots rise and Camelots fall."
James Bregman, 1964 first Olympic Judo team

When JFK was assassinated, Jackie Kennedy wrote a note to his trusted secretary. It read, "There will never be another Camelot."

When people are connected to an overarching mission, the sum is always greater than the parts. In 1992, *National Home Center News* wrote, "Home Depot is a place where individuals are trusted with great freedom, where personal and corporate growth are inextricable and where people believe they are part of an enterprise that is larger and more important than themselves. It is a place where ordinary people act extraordinarily."

Organizations go through life cycles of growth and maturation. As organizations grow and mature, they need different types of leaders at each life stage. But the stories that give a sense of the company history and culture live on. Seven years after I left Home Depot, I had lunch with a store associate. "Is it true?" she asked wistfully, "All of the stories they tell about Bernie and Arthur?" Depot was not Camelot but, for many years, it was perhaps as close as an imperfect company can come.

What is your foundation?

"If you believe in it, you are coming from the heart. It is not a power struggle but what you believe."
Roz Hobbs

The last question in my extensive interviews with executives and Olympians was, "What is your source of strength?" Hesitantly, almost apologetically, with only one exception, they referenced their faith.

Don Schneider of Schneider National spoke for several, "As I get older, I can express what drives me and makes me who I am. It is important to know the meaning of life. A lot of the things I do can have an impact on others and the quality of their life. Christ is our most important role model; he spent his life helping others.

The Christian values of teaching and being helpful to others are not contradictory to capitalism."

Your faith may have been shaken by a setback, by hypocrisy or by incidents in your life that you perceived as unfair. Even today, though my faith is weak and as tiny as a mustard seed, I keep asking for the strength to carry on my message.

My grandfather's picture sits on my fireplace mantel. It shows a strong, handsome man in the prime of his youth, frozen forever in sepia. In my second year of graduate work, I discovered that John Thornbury had studied at Western Teacher's College. Some 60 years later, by fate or coincidence, I studied at the same school, now called Western Kentucky University.

I have come home to Kentucky. I have heard my grandfather's call. In my family's long line of ministry, I was called, not to the ministry, but to the marketplace.

What does it mean to win your way?

There are no second chances in competition – only the roar of the crowd for the big throws. But the sports event is only a small part of how we live our life. You have a second chance, starting today.

Winning, your way, is not one chance but a life-long process. It starts with forgiving your mistakes and making peace with your past. It continues with being comfortable in your own skin, having a calmness of purpose, with being mentally, physically and emotionally fit. It is finding fulfillment and satisfaction from life and experiences outside of work and living a full life. It is listening for your call – and answering that call.

Winning reconciles the broad overlaps between courage, character and benevolence, because winning your way is about your whole life.

We can't all become charismatic leaders, the kind you would walk over hot coals or chew off your right arm to follow. But we can all lead from our core values. We can create a climate of courage and character where our people can put their values into practice in all parts of their lives.

Even if you have lost sight of the values that drew you to business, you can rediscover the inspiration that business has long forsaken in the name of short-term profits. You can draw from deep reserves for the stamina to make it through the second half of your career.

Winning is pushing past discouragement and the darkness of self-doubt to reach clarity on who you are and what you value. It is becoming a leader of great character.

Winning, your way

"Really, it is a wonderful thing to strive for Olympic Gold; to have and to pursue a dream; to know the exhilaration of competition and the intenseness of the moment, the sweet perfection of the perfect effortless throw. To know you did everything possible that you could to be the best you could be means life without regret. What more could one desire?"
Marissa Pedulla, 1996 Olympian

In the end, it is as easy as it is extremely difficult. In the end, it is only how you live your life that really matters. You can become the kind of leader people will talk about twenty years from now and pattern themselves after. You can use your platform for great good. You can pass down your hard-won wisdom and life lessons. You can make a great difference in your life, your children's lives and the lives of those you lead.

By living and leading with character you will look back without fear, knowing you gave your all. And you will know what it is like to win without losing your way.

Chapter Eight

Leadership Questions

- What is the most important lesson you have learned?

- What would you like to be remembered for?

- What is the source of your strength?

A final word to readers

This small, slim book that you hold in your hands is a message of hope. How you receive its message and apply it to your life will determine your outcome. Will you put it aside in a stack of briefly read business books? Or will you read and re-read it, highlighting and underlining sections, taking the time to work each exercise? Who will you make your accountability partner in your journey to become a leader of character?

This book will reach a wide readership through readers who believe in its message -pass this copy onto a friend or business colleague and make a difference.

How has this message impacted your life? We'd like to hear from you - visit us online at http://www.winningyourway.com to complete the reader feedback form, email us or contribute to future books in the Winning series.

This book begins and ends with Jeremy's story. Two weeks after the 9/11 tragedy I made a presentation in Columbus, Ohio. During the six hour drive, I debated whether to include the story of United Flight #93. I wasn't sure I could tell it without breaking down. I shared Jeremy's story and the audience shared my grief.

A year after 9/11 I no longer tell the now familiar story of United Flight #93. Instead, I dedicate each presentation to Jeremy's courage in life and death. A year after 9/11, a college professor who heard that first difficult presentation gives her students extra credit points for telling Jeremy's story. We have not forgotten.

A year after 9/11, baby Emerson is growing up. Donations to her college fund can be made to:

Emerson Glick
c/o Merrill Lynch
P.O. Box 911
Windham, NY 12496

Notes

Chapter 1

1. Ethic Resource Center, *2000 National Business Ethic Survey, Volume 1* (Washington D.C., Ethics Resource Center, 2000) page 11.
2. The John F. Kennedy Presidential Exhibition: Let us begin.
3. *The Economist* (May 16, 1992 Vol. 323, Issue 7759): 19.
4. Kurt Blumenau, "Doing the right thing" A *collection of news articles relating to the Center for Business Ethics,* April 09, 2001.
5. ibid
6. ibid
7. Ethic Resource Center, *2000 National Business Ethic Survey, Volume 1* (Washington D.C., Ethics Resource Center, 2000) page 39.
8. Steve Maynard, "Ethics programs in Tacoma, Washington" *The News Tribune,* 09 October 2000.
9. Ken Johnson, "Research and education pages" <http://www.ethicaledge.com>
10. Ethical Issues in the Employer-Employee Relationship; a survey sponsored by the Society of Financial Service Professionals in association with Walker Information, Inc. March 2001.
11. Clifton Leaf, "Send them to jail" *Fortune,* 18 March 2002, 62-78.

12.   Allan Sloan, "Who killed Enron" *Newsweek*, 21 January 2002, 19-24.
13.   Allan Sloan, "The Enron effect" *Newsweek*, 28 January 2002, 34-35.
14.   Allan Sloan, "Who killed Enron" *Newsweek*, 21 January 2002, 19-24.
15.   ibid
16.   Howard Fineman and Michael Isikoff, "Lights out: Enron's failed power play" *Newsweek,* 21, January, 2002, 15-18.
17.   Evan Thomas and Andrew Murr, "Who blew it all" *Newsweek,* 04, February 2002, 19-24.
18.   Clifton Leaf, "Send them to jail" *Fortune,* 18 March 2002, 62-78.

Chapter 2

1.   2000 Organizational Integrity Survey, KPMG, 1-4
2.   Jeffrey B. Caufaude, "Cultivating new leadership" *Association Management,* 52, (2000): 73
3.   ibid
4.   ibid
5.   ibid
6.   Amy Rottier, "Gen 2001: Loyalty and Values" *Workforce,* 80, no. 10 (2001):23
7.   Nancy Pekala, "Conquering the generational divide" *Journal of Property Management,* 66, no.6 (2001):30-37
8.   Jamie Swedberg, "Culture Shock" *Credit Union Management,* 24, no.5 (2001):32-33
9.   Brenton Faber, "Gen/Ethics" *Technical Communication Quarterly,* 10, no 3 (2001): 291-319.
10.   ibid
11.   Toddi Gutner, "A balancing act for Gen X women" *Business Week,* 21, January 2002, 82.

Chapter 3

1. Nancy Gibbs, "Making time for a baby" *Newsweek*, 15
    April 2002, 49-59.
2. ibid
3. ibid

Chapter 4

1. Ethic Resource Center, *2000 National Business Ethic
    Survey, Volume 1* (Washington D.C., Ethics Resource
    Center, 2000) page 30.
2. Ethic Resource Center, *2000 National Business Ethic
    Survey, Volume 1* (Washington D.C., Ethics Resource
    Center, 2000) page 15.
3. ibid
4. Ethic Resource Center, *2000 National Business Ethic
    Survey, Volume 1* (Washington D.C., Ethics Resource
    Center, 2000) page 14.
5. Ethic Resource Center, *2000 National Business Ethic
    Survey, Volume 1* (Washington D.C., Ethics Resource
    Center, 2000) page 33.
6. ibid
7. Ethic Resource Center, *2000 National Business Ethic
    Survey, Volume 1* (Washington D.C., Ethics Resource
    Center, 2000) page 27.
8. ibid
9. ibid
10. Allan Sloan, "The Enron effect" *Newsweek*, 28 January
    2002, 34-35.
11. Dennis K. Berman, Michael Schroeder and Shawn Young,
    "SEC probes Lucent accounting practices" *The Wall Street
    Journal*, 09 February 2001.
12. Mark Maremont and James Bandler, "Concession by Xerox
    may not satisfy the SEC" *The Wall Street Journal*, 01 June
    2001.

13. Ethical Issues in the Employer-Employee Relationship; a survey sponsored by the Society of Financial Service Professionals in association with Walker Information, Inc. March 2001.
14. Ethic Resource Center, *2000 National Business Ethic Survey, Volume 1* (Washington D.C., Ethics Resource Center, 2000) page 14.
15. Ethic Resource Center, *2000 National Business Ethic Survey, Volume 1* (Washington D.C., Ethics Resource Center, 2000) page 44.
16. Ethic Resource Center, *2000 National Business Ethic Survey, Volume 1* (Washington D.C., Ethics Resource Center, 2000) page 49.

Chapter 5

1.   Harriet Rubin, "The "S" word" *Fast Company,* March 2001, 44.
2.   Sue Shellenbarger, "Why many bosses need to alter their approach toward older workers" *The Wall Street Journal.*
3.   ibid
4.   ibid
5.   Steven Reiss, "Secrets of happiness" *Psychology Today*, January/February 2001, 50-56.
6.   ibid
7.   ibid
8.   Harold S. Kushner, *Living a life that matters* (New York: Random House, 2001), page 153.
9.   Mary Beth Marklein, "College grads bask in glow of service" *USA Today*, 30 May 2002.
10. Harold S. Kushner, *Living a life that matters* (New York: Random House, 2001), page 136.
11. Bob Buford, *Half Time* (Michigan: Zondervan Publishing House, 1994), page 160.
12. Juanelle Teague, "Turning Points" *Speaker DNA*, 2003, 16-24.

13.   ibid
14.   Bob Buford, *Half Time* (Michigan: Zondervan
      Publishing House, 1994), page 160.

Chapter 6

1.   Lee Hecht Harrison, *Please go, please stay* (Woodcliff
      Lake, NJ Lee Hecht Harrison 2000) page 1.
2.   ibid
3.   Robert Simons, Henry Mitzberg and Kunal Basu,
      "Memo to CEOs" *Fast Company,* June 2002.
4.   Lee Hecht Harrison, *Please go, please stay* (Woodcliff
      Lake, NJ Lee Hecht Harrison 2000) page 11.
5.   Lee Hecht Harrison, *Please go, please stay* (Woodcliff
      Lake, NJ Lee Hecht Harrison 2000) page 8.
6.   Lee Hecht Harrison, *Please go, please stay* (Woodcliff
      Lake, NJ Lee Hecht Harrison 2000) page 10.
7.   Robert Simons, Henry Mitzberg and Kunal Basu,
      "Memo to CEOs" *Fast Company,* June 2002.
8.   Lee Hecht Harrison, *Please go, please stay* (Woodcliff
      Lake, NJ, Lee Hecht Harrison 2000) page 12.
9.   Lee Hecht Harrison, *Beyond downsizing* (Woodcliff
      Lake, NJ, Lee Hecht Harrison 1997) page 2.
10.   Lee Hecht Harrison, *Please go, please stay* (Woodcliff
      Lake, NJ, Lee Hecht Harrison 2000) page 24.
11.   Robert Simons, Henry Mitzberg and Kunal Basu,
      "Memo to CEOs" *Fast Company,* June 2002.
12.   Lee Hecht Harrison, *Please go, please stay* (Woodcliff
      Lake, NJ, Lee Hecht Harrison 2000) page 24.
13.   Lee Hecht Harrison, *Beyond downsizing* (Woodcliff
      Lake, NJ, Lee Hecht Harrison 1997) page 8.
14.   Kemba J. Dunham, "Employers seek ways to lure back
      laid-off workers" *The Wall Street Journal,* 19 June
      2001
15.   ibid
16.   ibid
17.   ibid

18.   Lee Hecht Harrison, *Please go, please stay* (Woodcliff Lake, NJ, Lee Hecht Harrison 2000) page 8.

19.   Ethic Resource Center, *2000 National Business Ethic Survey, Volume 1* (Washington D.C., Ethics Resource Center, 2000) page 39.

20.   2000 Organizational Integrity Survey, KPMG. 1-4.

Chapter 7

1.   Paul Krugman, "Greed is bad" *The New York Times*, 4 June 2002.

2.   Allan Sloan, "WorldCom's wrong numbers" *Newsweek,* 8 July 2002.

3.   Howard Fineman, "The anxiety election" *Newsweek* , 21 October 2002.

4.   Allan Sloan and Johnnie L. Roberts, "Sticky business" *Newsweek*, 22, July 2002.

5.   ibid

6.   Clifton Leaf, "Send them to jail" *Fortune,* 18 March 2002, 62-78.

7.   Paul Krugman, "Greed is bad" *The New York Times*, 4 June 2002.

8.   Allan Sloan, "WorldCom's wrong numbers" *Newsweek,* 8 July 2002.

9.   Jane Bryant Quinn, "Now who do you trust?" Newsweek, 27, May 2002.

10.   Christine Canabou, Erika Germer and Heath Row, "Speedmeter" *Fast Company,* September 2002.

11.   Allan Sloan, "Think globally, skip tax locally" *Newsweek*, 03, June 2002.

12.   Devin Leonard, "The Adelphia story" *Fortune,* 12 August 2002.

13.   Kurt Blumenau, "Doing the right thing" A *collection of news articles relating to the Center for Business Ethics,* April 09, 2001.

14.   Milton Friedman, *Capitalism and freedom* (Chicago: University of Chicago Press, 1962).

15. Robert Simons, Henry Mitzberg and Kunal Basu, "Memo to CEOs" *Fast Company,* June 2002.
16. Jane Bryant Quinn, "In search of clean stocks" *Newsweek,* 10 June 2002.
17. ibid
18. ibid
19. Robert Simons, Henry Mitzberg and Kunal Basu, "Memo to CEOs" *Fast Company,* June 2002.
20. Jane Bryant Quinn, "In search of clean stocks" *Newsweek,* 10 June 2002
21. Robert Simons, Henry Mitzberg and Kunal Basu, "Memo to CEOs" *Fast Company,* June 2002.
22. Clifton Leaf, "Send them to jail" *Fortune,* 18 March 2002, 62-78.

Chapter 8

1. Harold S. Kushner, *Living a life that matters* (New York: Random House, 2001), page 6.